CW00468119

CONTENTS

ACKNOWLEDGEMENTS

Many thanks do my dear sister Mary who so helpfully and patiently listened to each Psalm as I put them into rhyme.

Many thanks to dear Pam and Dave Nickson who have continually encouraged me to write my books, for editing and helping me to publish them.

I do pray that you the reader will be truly blessed by this book and be encouraged to read the bible for yourself.

God bless,

Trish Bishop

BOOK 1

Psalms 1-41 v 13

PSALM 1

"Blessed is the man who,
Keeps away from those who sin,
And those who are scorners too,
The Law of God his delight is in,
Is what I write to you.

He stays in it day and night,
Like a tree planted by a river,
He shall always bear much fruit,
And his leaves shall never wither.

Yes his season is always fruitful,
And he will prosper in all he does,
For day and night he meditates,
In the Law of God he loves.

The ungodly really are not so,
The Law of God they do not cherish,
Like the chaff that blows away in the wind,
Their way will always perish."

PSALM 2

"Why do nations and Kings so rage,
Against the Lord and His anointed Son,
Casting away all that joined them together,
All bonds and cords every one?

The Lord who sits in heaven shall bitterly laugh,
Filled with wrath is He,
He will speak in His displeasure,
"I will set My King on the Hill of Zion He will be."

This decree the Lord has shared,
"Today You are My begotten Son,
The nations and whole earth will be Yours,
You will break into pieces every one."

Therefore be wise you Kings and Judges of the earth,
Because the Son, angry is He,
His wrath is but a little so put your trust in Him,
And safe you will always be."

PSALM 3

"Lord there are so many against me that say,
"There is no help from God for him."
But instead You oh Lord are a shield for me,
My glory and the lifter of my head.

I cried to the Lord and He heard me,
Then I lay down and slept,
Though ten thousand be against me,
The Lord sustained and safe me kept.

Oh God you have saved me now,
All my enemies struck on the cheekbone,
You have broken the teeth of the ungodly,
Salvation and blessing for your people alone."

PSALM 4

"Hear me when I call to You,
'Oh God relieve me in my distress,'
Have mercy and hear my prayer,
Then me You will always bless.

"You sons of men how long,
Will you turn My glory to shame?
How long will you lie and be worthless?"
God has saved the godly and will hear me again.

Be angry and do not sin,
Meditate on your bed and be still,
Offer up the sacrifice of righteousness,
Putting trust in the Lord and His will.

Lord let Your face shine upon us,
''Who will do us good?'' many say,
You have put gladness in my heart,
And taken all sadness away.

Now for more than just a season,
Their grain and wine increase,
And now I lay down in safety,
Having a good sleep in peace."

PSALM 5

"Give ear to my words O Lord,
Consider my meditation every day,
Give heed to my cry my King and God,
For to You only do I pray.

You are a God that takes no pleasure in wickedness,
Nor does evil fit well with You,
You hate all the boastful and deceitful,
And all that the bloodthirsty do.

As for me I will come into Your house,
Worshipping in Your Temple I will be,
Lead me O Lord in Your righteousness,
Keeping me so safe from my enemy.

There is no faithfulness in their mouth,
Full of destruction in their inward parts,
Their throats are like an open tomb,
As they flatter with their tongue all hearts.

Pronounce them guilty O God,
Let them fall by counsels all their own,
Cast them out in their transgressions,
For rebellion to You they have shown.

But allow all who trust in You,
Shout for joy because them You defend,
And let all those who love Your name,

Be joyful in You until the end.

For You O Lord will always bless,
The righteous, who to You yield,
For You will bless and surround,
Them all as with a loving shield."

PSALM 6

"O Lord do not in displeasure and anger rebuke me,
Have mercy for I am weak,
For my bones and my soul are troubled in me,
For, 'How long?' Lord is the answer I seek.

Return O Lord and deliver me,
For Your mercy's sake, me save,
Death will have no remembrance of You,
There will be no thanks in the grave.

I am weary with my groaning,
All night I make my bed to swim,
This is all because of my enemies,
My eye wastes because of tears and the grief I am in.

The Lord has heard my supplication,
And the voice of my weeping too,
Let my enemies be ashamed and troubled O Lord,
For You have heard my prayer to You."

PSALM 7

"O Lord save me from those who persecute,
Because only in You do I trust,
If I have caused evil to one with me at peace,
Then let him trample my life in the dust.

Arise O Lord, lift Yourself up in anger,
And for the judgement You have commanded for me,
Let the congregation of people that You surround,
Return on high O Lord to judge my integrity.

Let the wickedness of the wicked come to an end,
The hearts and minds of the just, God does test,
God saves also the upright of heart,
So my defenses of God are at rest.

God is angry with the wicked every day,
He will not turn for as judge He is just,
He will sharpen the sword and bow,
For to get ready for battle He must.

Behold the wicked bring forth iniquity,
Into the pit he dug he fell down,
His iniquity will return to his own head,
When violence comes down like a crown.

I will praise the Lord at all times,
Because of His righteousness is why,
I will sing to Him all praises,

For His name is the Lord Most High."

PSALM 8

"O Lord our Lord above the heavens,
How excellent that the mouths of babes,
And infants tell your story,
You have all strength against your enemies,
Against the avenger You show Your glory.

When I survey the heavens,
And all Your hands have made,
The moon and stars and the son of man also,
You made him a little lower than the angels,
Gave him dominion and told him to go,
And be in charge of the works of Your hands.

To take care of oxen, beasts and sheep,
To also watch over the fish in the sea,
And the birds of the air to safe keep.

Your name O Lord is above the earth,
Above all the heavens too,
What is man that You even think of him,
And allow him to work with You?"

PSALM 9

"I will praise You O Lord with all my heart,
And tell of all the marvellous work You do,
I will sing praise to Your name Most High,
For I am glad to rejoice in You.

My enemies turn back again,
In Your presence they all do perish,
You sit on Your throne to judge righteousness,
My cause and right You do cherish.

You have rebuked nations O God,
Destroyed the wicked with a shout,
The work of the enemy is finished forever,
Their name You have blotted out.

You have destroyed many cities,
Even the memory of them is gone,
But You O Lord endure forever,
Your judgement will cure all that is wrong.

You O Lord are a refuge for all the oppressed,
In times of trouble they depend on You,
Those who know Your name do trust,
You will not forsake them in all You do.

Sing praises to the Lord in Zion,
Among the people declare all His deeds,
He avenges blood and remembers them,

Taking care of the humble and all his needs.

Have mercy on me O Lord,
See all those who do me hate,
You will lift me up from death,
And I praise at Zion's gate.

Yes I will rejoice in Your salvation,
The nations have dug and sink in the pit,
Their feet are caught in the net they hid,
They laid a trap and have fallen in it.

The wicked shall be turned into hell,
And the nations that God will forget,
But the needy will not be forgotten,
All the supply they expect they will get.

Arise O Lord do not let man prevail,
Let the nations be judged in Your sight,
Put mere man into fear O Lord,
So all nations may do what is right."

PSALM 10

"Why do You stand afar off O Lord?
In times of trouble why do You hide?
Let the wicked be caught in his own plots,
For he persecutes the poor in his pride.

The wicked blesses the greedy but renounces the Lord,
Of his own desires constantly speak,
God will not ever be in his thoughts,
For God's face he does not seek.

His ways are always prospering,
God's laws are out of his sight,
He sneers at all his enemies,
And says, "I will win every fight."

He boasts, "I shall never be moved,
I in adversity shall never be."
His mouth is full of cursing and deceit,
Under his tongue is trouble and iniquity.

He sits in lurking places of villages,
In secret a murderer of the innocent is he,
His eyes are fixed on the helpless,
Waiting like a lion in his den he will be.

He lies in wait to catch the poor,
They falling helpless into his net will be,
He says in his heart, "God has forgotten,

For He hides His face and won't see."

Arise O Lord lift up Your hand,
Save the humble from this one's heart,
O why do the wicked renounce You God?
He believes You do not have a part.

But You have seen, You see trouble and grief,
The helpless commits himself for You to repay,
You break the arm of the wicked man,
Seek out his wickedness until all gone away.

The Lord is King forever and ever,
The nations perish out of His hand,
You prepare the heart of the oppressed and humble,
You hear and keep them safe in Your hand."

PSALM 11

"As I trust the Lord, how can I say to my soul,
'Like a bird to your mountain flee,'
For the wicked make ready the arrow,
To shoot the upright secretly.

The Lord is in His Holy Temple,
His throne behind heaven's gates,
The Lord sees and tests the righteous,
The wicked who love violence He hates.

On the wicked He will rain coals,
Filled with fire and brimstone so bright,
For the Lord who loves righteousness is righteous,
His face always beholds the upright."

PSALM 12

"Help Lord, for the godly man ceases,
We find none faithful though we seek,
They speak idle words to a neighbour,
With flattering lips and double heart speak.

May the Lord cut off all flattering lips,
For those with proud tongues have said,
"With our tongues we will prevail,
Who is Lord now over our heads?"

For the oppression of the poor and needy, -
"Now I will arise," the Lord says,
"I will set him in the safety he yearns,
And keep him safe in all of his ways."

"The words of the Lord are pure words,
Like silver tried seven times in furnaces of earth,
You Lord will preserve and keep them,
Safe in You for all of their worth.
The wicked prowl on every side,
Violence is exalted by all men."

These are all truths the Psalmist has said,
That is why these rhymes I do pen - *Trish Bishop*

27

PSALM 13

"How long O Lord? Will you forget me forever?
How long will You hide Your face from me?
How long will I listen to the thoughts in my heart?
How long O Lord will my enemy exalted be?

Consider and hear me O Lord my God,
Enlighten my eyes lest I sleep the sleep of death,
Do not let my enemy prevail over me,
Nor rejoice against me with every breath.

But I will trust always in Your mercy,
In Your salvation my heart will rejoice,
Because the Lord deals well with me,
I will sing praises with all of my voice."

PSALM 14

"A fool says in his heart, "There is no God!"
Repent of all that he says he should,
For abominable works they all do,
There are none that do any good.

The Lord looks down from heaven,
To see what the children of men have done,
There are none who seek or understand God,
There are none who do good not one.

"Have all the workers of iniquity no knowledge,
Who eat up My people like bread?"
They do not call upon the Lord,
But are filled with much fear and dread.

God is with the righteous,
You shame the talk of the poor,
The Lord will be the poor's refuge,
Not one could ask for more.

Oh that the salvation of Israel,
Would from Zion come out,
When the Lord brings back the captivity,
Israel and Jacob will rejoice with a shout."

PSALM 15

"Lord, who may abide in Your Tabernacle?
Who may dwell on Your Holy Hill?
He who walks with upright and truth in his heart,
Nor backbites his neighbour most certainly will.

He does not reproach a friend either,
Vile persons he does always despise,
He honours those who fear the Lord,
He does good to all who to Him cries.

He does not put his money to credit,
Nor against the innocent a bribe take,
Because he does all these good things,
His sure foundation will not shake."

PSALM 16

"Preserve me O God for I trust in You,
My goodness is nothing without Your right,
For all the saints upon this earth,
Are the excellent ones in whom You delight.

Their sorrows will be multiplied,
Who seek other gods to their shame,
Their sacrifices of blood I will not offer,
Nor take on my lips their name.

O Lord You are my portion and cup,
In my inheritance You maintain my lot,
I have all in pleasant places,
You have given me all I have got.

I will bless the Lord for His counsel,
My heart instructs me while I sleep,
Because the lord is at my right hand,
I will not move if before me the Lord I keep.

Therefore my glory and heart are glad,
My flesh does hope and rejoice,
You will not leave my soul in Sheol,
To allow Your holy one corruption is not Your choice.

You will show me the very path of life,
The way You show I will always employ,
In Your right hand are many pleasures,

In Your presence is fullness of joy."

PSALM 17

"Hear a just cause O Lord,
Give ear to lips good in Your sight,
My vindication comes from Your presence,
Let Your eyes look on things upright.

You test my heart and visit me in the night,
You have tried me and found in me no wrong,
I will keep my lips clean and away from the destroyer,
So my steps will not slip my footsteps steady and strong.

I call upon You and You hear me O God,
Incline Your ear and hear all my speech,
Show loving kindness by Your right hand,
To all who trust and believe all You teach.

From the wicked who oppress me,
Keep me as the apple of Your eye,
Hide me under the shadow of Your wings,
And let my deadly enemy pass by.

They have closed up their hearts against You,
With their mouths they speak with pride,
They are like a lion eager to tear his prey,
While the young lions lurk and hide.

Arise O Lord and cast them down,
Deliver me from their wicked sword,
With Your hand from the men in this life,

Whose belly You have filled O Lord.

They are satisfied with children,
And the hidden treasures that You gave,
They have a portion in this life,
Leaving the rest of possessions to a babe."

PSALM 18

"I will love You O Lord my strength,
My God in whom I do trust,
You are my salvation and stronghold,
To call on You and praise You I must.

The pangs of death and ungodly men surround me,
The sorrows of Sheol and the snares of death,
I cried out in my distress as death confronted me,
And God heard from His Temple my voice,
What could have been my last breath.

The earth shook and trembled and the hills quaked,
Devouring fire came down from an angry God's mouth,
As upon the wings of the wind and a cherub He flew,
The Lord thundered from heaven in the dark clouds,
Bringing darkness and hailstones He did do.

The Lord Most High uttered His voice,
With hailstones, fire and arrows He scattered the foe,
At Your rebuke O Lord and the blast of Your breath,
You delivered me and my enemies had to go.

They had confronted me in the days of my calamity,
But the Lord moved me to a safe place to be,
He was all the support that I needed,
His deliverance was because He delighted in me.

The Lord has rewarded my righteousness,

According to the cleanness of my hands,
I have always kept the way of the Lord,
His statute and judgement in me always stands.

O Lord with the merciful You show mercy,
With the devious, shrewdness You will show,
You will always save the humble,
Those who are haughty will have to go.

The Lord will light a lamp in my darkness,
By my God any troop I can face,
And I can leap over any wall,
For I do all this by God's grace.

He is a shield to all who trust in Him,
A perfect way to me He does show,
He makes my feet like the feet of a deer,
So that in all high places I can go.

I have pursued and overtaken my enemies,
Did not turn until all of them I did defeat,
They are wounded and cursed and cannot arise,
For all have fallen under my feet.

You have given me the neck of my enemies,
I have dismayed all who hated me,
They cried to the Lord but He did not answer,
I beat them so like dust and dirt they will be.

You delivered me from the striving of people,
Of the nations You have made me the head,
As soon as they hear they always obey me,
And foreigners fade away in fear and dread.

The Lord lives and blessed is my Rock,
Let the Lord of my salvation be exalted by me,
He delivers me from all of my enemies,
Safe from the violence of man I will be.

I will to You among the gentiles give thanks,
And always sing praises to Your name,
For You have given deliverance to Your King,
And mercy to David and his descendants the same."

PSALM 19

"The heavens declare the Glory of the Lord,
The firmament shows handiwork and utters speech,
And night unto night reveals knowledge,
Their voice in every language do reach.

There is no place that their voice is not heard,
Throughout the earth gone out has their line,
Their words to the ends of the earth,
Will go on till the ends of time.

The Law of the Lord is perfect converting the soul,
The testimony of the Lord makes the simple wise,
His statutes are right and rejoicing the heart,
His commandments enlightening the eyes.

The fear of the Lord is enduring and clean,
The judgments of the Lord are righteous and true,
Sweeter than a honeycomb and to be desired like gold,
As they keep them, Your servants rewarding You do.

Who understands his faults and errors?
Do not let sin have dominion over me,
Then I shall always be blameless,
Innocent of transgression I shall be.

Let the words of my mouth, the meditation of my heart,
Be always acceptable in Your sight,
For You O Lord are my Redeemer,

In Your strength I am filled with might."

PSALM 20

"May the Lord answer you in the day of trouble,
May the name of the God of Jacob defend you,
May He send help from the Sanctuary,
And He will remember the offerings you do.

May He strengthen you out of Zion,
Be with you in all that you do,
May your burnt sacrifice be accepted,
And give all your hearts desires to you.

We will rejoice in our salvation,
Set up our banners in God's name,
May the Lord fill our petitions,
He will answer from heaven again.

Now I know the Lord saves His anointed,
But those who trust in chariots and horses,
Will be bowed and fall down,
But if we arise and all stand upright,
In our Lord and King, the answer is found."

PSALM 21

"The king shall have joy in Your strength O Lord,
In Your salvation greatly rejoice,
You have given him his heart's desires,
You have listened to the requests from his voice.

You meet him with blessings and goodness,
You have set a pure gold crown on his head,
When death threatened he asked You for life,
You gave him length of days and life's bread.

You have made him most blessed forever,
In Your presence he is exceedingly glad,
The king trusts in the Lord for His mercy,
In the Most High he will never be sad.

Your hand will find Your enemies,
Your right hand will find those who hate You,
The Lord shall swallow them up in wrathful fire,
They will be as a fiery oven, that is true.

Their offspring and descendants You will destroy,
For they intended evil against You,
Therefore You made them turn their back,
Making arrows in their face You did do."

PSALM 22

"My God, my God why have You me forsaken?
Why do You not hear my plea?
Why are You so far from giving me help,
When I cry in the day You don't hear me?

You are Holy and enthroned in Israel's praise,
Our fathers to deliver them trusted You,
They cried to You and You delivered,
Shaming them You did not do.

You have formed me in my mother's womb,
From my birth I was given to You,
And You have always been my God,
Keeping me safe is what You always do.

Oh be my strength and hasten to help me,
Deliver me from the dog and the sword,
Save me from the lion's mouth and wild oxen,
Do not be far away from me O Lord.

You who fear the Lord praise Him,
Declare His name to your brothers too,
In the midst of an assembly praise,
Fear Him descendants of Jacob all of you.

My praise shall be in the great assembly,
For the poor will eat and satisfied will be,
I will pay my vows before those who fear God,

When you seek Him He will set your heart free!"

This psalm is all about Jesus the Christ,
All that happened before on the cross He died,
I did not want to put all of that into rhyme
Please go to your bible and in Psalm 22 abide.

God Bless.
Trish x

PSALM 23

"The Lord is my shepherd I shall not want,
He leads me by waters so still,
I am made to lie down in green pastures,
To restore in me righteousness is His will.

For though I walk through the shadow of death,
You are there so evil does not touch me,
You prepare a table before my enemies,
Your rod and staff my comfort shall be.

You anoint my head with oil,
Surely goodness and mercy follow me,
All the days of my life, my cup runs over,
Dwelling in the Lord's house I will be."

PSALM 24

"The earth is the Lord's in all its fullness,
For He has founded it upon the sea,
He has established it on the waters,
In the world His will always shall be.

Who may ascend into the hill of the Lord,
Who in His Holy place stands?
He who has not worshipped idols,
And has a pure heart and clean hands.

The righteous from the God of his salvation,
Are the generation of Jacob's own race,
The Lord has filled with goodness,
All who will seek His face.

Who is the King of Glory?
The Lord mighty in battle is He,
Lift up you everlasting doors,
And the King of Glory you will see."

PSALM 25

"To You O Lord I lift up my soul,
Unashamed O God I trust in You,
Let no my enemies triumph over me,
Let be ashamed all who treacherous things do.

Show me Your way O Lord,
Your paths of truth to me teach,
You are the God of my salvation,
Your standards I will surely reach.

Remember O Lord Your kindness and mercy,
Remember not my transgressions and sin,
According to Your mercy remember me,
Then Your loving goodness I shall be in.

Good and upright is our Lord,
He teaches sinners and the humble His way,
All the paths of the Lord are mercy and truth,
So keep His covenant and testimonies each day.

Who is the man who fears the Lord?
He will teach him in His choice of way,
He will live in good prosperity,
His descendants on the earth will stay.

The secrets of the Lord are with those who fear Him,
His covenant to them He will show,
My eyes are ever with the Lord,

For out of the net my feet will go.

Turn O Lord and have mercy on me,
For I am desolate and afflicted too,
Consider my enemies for they are many,
I, O Lord will trust and wait for You."

PSALM 26

"Vindicate me O Lord for I walk in integrity,
Examine me O Lord and prove me,
My trust in You keeps me from slipping,
Your loving kindness I will always see.

I do not sit with idolatrous mortals,
In Your truth I will always walk,
I hate the assembly of evildoers,
And with the wicked I will not talk.

I will go about Your Altar O Lord,
In innocence I will wash my hands,
I will tell of all Your wondrous works,
For I love Your house where Your Glory stands.

Do not gather my soul with sinners,
Nor my life with bloodthirsty men,
In whose hands are sinister schemes,
And those who offer bribes to them.

But as for me I will walk in integrity,
Redeem me and be merciful to me,
My feet will always be in a firm place,
In the congregation, the Lord blessed will be."

PSALM 27

"The Lord is my light and my salvation,
With His strength, whom shall I fear?
My enemies and foes stumbled and fell,
To encamp against me cost them dear.

One thing I have desired of the Lord,
That I might dwell in His house, I seek,
To inquire in His Temple when in trouble,
For He will hide me when I am weak.

My head shall be lifted up above my enemies,
That are encamped all around me,
I will offer sacrifices of joy in the Temple,
Singing praises I will always be.

Hear O Lord when I cry with my voice,
Have mercy and answer me,
You have told me to seek Your face,
Seeking Your face I always will be.

Do not hide Your face O Lord,
Do not turn your servant in anger away,
Though my father and mother forsake me,
You Lord take care of me every day.

Teach me Your way O Lord, make my path smooth,
Do not deliver me to enemies that violence breathed,
When I could see amongst the living God's goodness,

I would have lost heart had I not believed.

Wait on the Lord be of good courage,
For He shall strengthen your heart,
So wait on the Lord I always say,
If you do you will have a good start."

PSALM 28

"To you I will cry O Lord my Rock,
I will be lost if You are silent to me,
Hear my voice when I cry to you,
Lifting hands in Your sanctuary I will be.

Do not take me away with wicked,
And the workers of iniquity,
Who speak peace with evil hearts,
Let their reward according to their evil be.

Blessed is the Lord for He has heard me,
The Lord is my strength and shield,
My heart trusted in Him and He helped me,
With joy to Him my praises I will yield.

The Lord is the strength of His anointed,
In a safe refuge them He does keep,
Saving His people and His inheritance,
Like a good shepherd looks after his sheep."

PSALM 29

"Give unto the Lord you mighty ones,
The strength and Glory due to His name,
Worship the Lord in the beauty of holiness,
Let His glory be ever the same.

The voice of the Lord is over the waters,
The voice of the Lord is powerful as can be,
The Lord is over many, many waters,
The voice of the Lord is full of Majesty.

The voice of the Lord breaks the cedars,
Yes He splinters the cedars of Lebanon,
He makes them also skip like a calf,
Like wild ox in Lebanon and Sirion.

The voice of the Lord shakes the wilderness,
The Lord the wilderness of Kadesh also shakes,
Strips the forest bare, and those in the Temple say, "Glory,"
The voice of the Lord, the deer to give birth makes."

PSALM 30

"I will exalt You O Lord, You have lifted me up,
You have not let my enemies rejoice over me,
I cried to You and You did heal,
My soul up from the grave will ever be.

Sing praises to the Lord you all His saints,
Give thanks remembering His Holy name,
For His anger is but for a moment,
If you weep in the night,
You will have joy in the morning again.

In my prosperity I said, 'I shall never be moved.'
Lord You made my mountain strong to stand,
You hid Your face so I was troubled,
Are our fathers still sitting by Your right hand?

I cried to the Lord and made supplication,
If to the pit I go down will the dust praise You?
Will it tell You the truth? Oh Lord have mercy on me,
You are my help and refuge in trouble that is true.

You have turned my mourning into dancing,
You have put off my sackcloth so I won't be sad,
To the end that my glory will sing praises to You,
To give thanks forever will make me glad."

PSALM 31

"In You O Lord do I put my trust,
Let me not be ashamed, set me free,
Be my rock and fortress of defense,
My rock of refuge always be.

Therefore Lord for Your name's sake,
Lead and guide me against my enemy,
Pull me from the net they in secret laid,
For You are my strength and will always be.

I have hated those who worship idols,
My trust and rejoicing is in Your mercy,
You have known me in all of my trouble,
And always helped in my adversity.

Have mercy O Lord I am in trouble,
My eye wastes away full of grief,
My life is spent with grief and my soul with sighing,
My strength fails and I look to You for relief.

I am a reproach among all my enemies,
Among all of my neighbours too,
I am repulsive to the people I know,
From me they run away it is true.

I am forgotten like a dead man,
There is fear and slander on every side,
And while they counsel against me,

I have nothing to do but to hide.

But as for me I will trust You,
You are my God I do say,
My times and life are in Your hand,
For You chase all my enemies away.

Do not let me be ashamed O Lord,
Let the wicked be as silent as the grave,
For they are insolent and contemptuous,
Speaking proudly against the righteous is how they behave.

O how great is You goodness O Lord,
Laid up for those who fear You,
You hide them secretly in Your presence,
Blessed are You Lord in all that You do.

You have shown kindness in a strong city,
In haste I said, 'I am cut off from Your eyes,'
But You heard the voice of my supplication,
Yes in love and mercy You heard my cries.

O love the Lord all you saints,
For He preserves the faithful and just,
He will repay the proud person,
Strengthening all who in the Lord do trust."

PSALM 32

"Blessed is he whose sin is forgiven,
Blessed is the man who has a clean sheet,
For the Lord has not imputed them to him,
And in his spirit there is no deceit.

When I kept silent my bones grew old,
Though I was groaning all of the day,
Day and night Your hand was heavy on me,
I was dried up in every way.

I acknowledged my sin to You O Lord,
My transgressions I have not hidden,
I have said I will confess to the Lord,
And by His grace I am forgiven.

For this cause, all the godly pray to You,
In the time that You may be found,
You are my hiding place O Lord,
And with songs of deliverance, me surround."

"I will instruct and teach you," says the Lord,
"In the ways that you should go,
I will guide you with My eye,
Do not ways of horses and mules show.

For they do not have understanding,
And must be led with a bit and bridle too,
For they have to have them fitted on,

Or they will not come near or be led by you."

"Many sorrows are due the wicked but,
In he who trusts the Lord's mercy has a part,
So be glad and rejoice all you righteous,
Shout with joy and with an upright heart."

PSALM 33

"Rejoice in the Lord O you righteous,
Praise from the upright is beautiful praise,
Make melody with the harp of ten strings,
With a shout of joy your voice raise.

For the word of the Lord is right and truth,
By His word all the heavens were made,
And all the hosts by the breath of His mouth,
The seas waters are in storehouses laid.

Let all the earth fear the Lord in awe,
For as He spoke all creation was done,
He brings the counsel of nations to nothing,
Their plans have no effect not one.

The Lord from heavens sees the sons of men,
From the place of His dwelling He did look,
As He fashions one by one all of their hearts,
All of consideration of their works He took.

No king is saved by the multitude of an army,
Strength cannot save a mighty man,
A horse is a vain hope for safety,
To deliver by strength not even a horse can.

Behold the eye of the Lord is on those who fear Him,
Who are hoping for His mercy it is true,
To deliver them from the hands of death,

And keep them from hunger too.

The Lord is our help and shield,
Our hearts will rejoice and trust too,
Because of the Lord's most Holy name,
Send Your mercy O Lord for our hope is in You."

PSALM 34

"I will bless the Lord at all times,
In my mouth will be continued praise,
My soul will make its boast in the Lord,
The humble with me in exaltation His name raise.

O taste and see that the Lord is good,
Fear and trust in Him all you saints,
Those who seek the Lord are never in want,
While the young lions in hunger waits.

Who is the man who seeks life,
Loves many days that he will see good?
Keep your tongue from evil and deceit,
Seek peace and not evil you should.

The eyes of the Lord are on the righteous,
And His ears are open to their cry,
The face of the Lord is against the evildoers,
For they trouble the righteous that's why.

The righteous cry out and the Lord hears,
He is near to all with a broken heart,
He delivers them out of their trouble,
Those with a contrite spirit also take part.

Many are the afflictions of the righteous,
But the Lord delivers them out of it all,
Not one of His bones shall be broken,

Those who hate the righteous shall fall.

Evil shall always slay the wicked,
But the Lord redeems His servants in the end,
None of the people who trust in Him,
Will He ever, ever condemn."

PSALM 35

"Plead my cause O Lord with those who strive,
With shield and buckler, fight those who fought me,
Stand and draw a spear for my help,
And stop the pursuing of my enemy.

Let them be brought to shame and dishonor,
Bring to confusion all who seek my life,
Let their way be dark and slippery,
For they are causing me so much strife.

Let the angel of the Lord pursue them,
For they have hidden a net for me in a pit,
Which they have dug to take my life,
O Lord let them themselves fall in it.

And my soul shall be joyful in the Lord,
For salvation my soul rejoices in Him,
You save the poor from he who plunders,
Delivering them from the trouble they are in.

Fierce witnesses rise up, to the sorrow of my soul,
Asking me things I do not know,
They have given me only evil,
For all the good I did show.

But as for me when they were sick,
I prayed and paced as though for a brother,
My clothing sackcloth and also fasting,

Bowed down as though for a mother.

They gathered and rejoiced in my adversity,
Against me their attacks did not cease,
They gnashed at me with their teeth,
Like ungodly mockers at a feast.

How long Lord will You look at my destruction?
Rescue me from the lions who want my life,
I will give You thanks in the great assembly,
And praise for my deliverance from strife.

Let them not rejoice who are my enemies,
Do not let them wink who wrongfully hate me,
They do not speak peace and are deceitful,
Laughing with their mouths against me they will be.

Do not be silent O Lord, for You have seen this,
O Lord awake and be always near to me,
Vindicate me according to Your righteousness,
O God, let them Your salvation of me see.

Do not let them rejoice over me O Lord,
'We have swallowed him up,' let them not say,
Put them into shame and confusion,
With dishonor take them all away.

Let those who favour me shout for joy,
'For the Lord be magnified,' they all say,
For He has pleasure that His servant prospers,
I will praise and speak of Your righteousness every day."

PSALM 36

"In my heart are thoughts on the wickedness of man,
The fear of God is not before his eyes,
He is full of wickedness and deceit,
In iniquity and hate he is not wise.

Your mercy O Lord is in the heavens,
Your faithfulness reaches the clouds above,
Your judgements are great and deep,
O Lord You preserve man and beast with love.

How precious is Your loving kindness O God,
The children of men trust under the shadow of Your wing,
You give them drink from the river of Your pleasures,
For Your fountain of life makes their hearts sing.

O continue Your loving kindness to those who know You,
And Your righteousness to the upright of heart,
Let not the foot of pride come against me,
Let not the hand of the wicked drive us apart."

PSALM 37

"Do not fret because of evildoers,
Envy not the workers of iniquity,
For they will soon be cut down like grass,
Their fate like the withering herb will be.

Trust in the Lord and do good,
In the land, on His faithfulness feed,
Delight yourself also in the Lord,
Receive the desires of your heart when Him you heed.

Commit your way to the Lord,
He shall bring forth your righteousness as light,
Trust Him and He will bring to pass,
Your justice in the noon day not the night.

Rest in the Lord and wait patiently for Him,
Do not fret over him who prospers in his way,
Because of the man who brings wicked schemes to pass,
Do not fret but put wrath and anger away.

For evildoers shall be cut off,
But those who wait on the Lord inherit the earth,
For yet in a little while, the wicked will be no more,
Though you look for him with all of your worth.

But the meek shall inherit the earth,
And delight in the abundance of peace,
The wicked plots against the just,

Gnashing at him and will not cease.

The Lord laughs at the wicked ones,
For He sees the coming of their day,
Though they cast down the poor and needy,
Their own bow and sword will turn them away.

A little that a righteous man has,
Is better than many a wicked man does hold,
For the arms of the wicked shall be broken,
But the righteous of the Lord shall be bold.

The Lord knows the days of the upright,
Their inheritance shall always be,
In days of famine they will be satisfied,
The Lord's enemies will surely flee.

The wicked borrow and do not repay,
But the righteous show mercy and give,
Those blessed by the Lord inherit the earth,
Those who He curses shall not live.

The steps of a good man are ordered by the Lord,
Who delights in his way in the land,
Though he falls he is not utterly cast down,
For the Lord upholds him with His hand.

I have been young and now am old,
Yet not have the righteous forsaken seen,
Nor his descendants begging for bread,
His descendants have always blessed been.

Mark the blameless man, observe the upright too,
For the future of both of them is peace,
But transgressors together shall be destroyed,
And their future forever on the decrease.

The salvation of the righteous is from the Lord,
He is their strength in times that trouble them,

Also because they put their trust in Him,
The power of the wicked over them will end."

PSALM 38

"O Lord do not rebuke me in Your wrath,
For Your arrows deeply pierce,
Nor chasten me in hot displeasure,
Your hand pressing down is fierce.

There is no soundness in my flesh,
Because You are angry with me,
Nor any health in my bones,
My sin and iniquity over my head will be.

Like a heavy burden too heavy for me,
My wounds are foul and festering to see,
Because of my foolishness I am so troubled,
Bowed down and mourning greatly.

Lord all my desire is before You,
You hear my sighing all day long,
My heart pants my strength fails me,
The light of my eyes also is gone.

Those who seek my life plan deception,
But like a deaf man I do not hear,
I am like a mute who cannot open his mouth,
Deaf and mute I am because of fear.

But in You O Lord I put my hope,
You will hear O Lord God my plea,
Lest they rejoice over me hear O Lord,

When my foot slips they exalt over me.

I am ready to fall, my sorrow always before me,
I am in anguish over my sin,
But my enemies are vigorous and strong,
They are my adversaries for the good I am in.

Do not forsake me O Lord,
O my God be not far from me,
O Lord of my salvation ,
Make haste and my helper be."

PSALM 39

"I will restrain my mouth with a muzzle,
Guarding my ways lest with my tongue I sin,
While the wicked are before me,
I was silent but filled with anger within.

Then I spoke with my tongue,
'Lord make me to know my end,
What is the measure of my days?
An answer to me dear Lord please send.'

Indeed my days are but a hands breath,
My age is nothing before You,
Every man in his state is but a vapour,
Even so their hope is in You.

And now O Lord what do I wait for?
For my hope is in You too,
Deliver me from my transgressors,
So that good is all I shall do.

Do not make me the reproach of the foolish,
I am consumed by the blow of Your hand,
In correcting man for iniquity his beauty melts,
With rebuke he becomes a vapour of a man.

Hear my prayer O Lord do not be silent,
Do not be silent at my every tear,
Remove Your gaze so I regain strength,

Before my time comes and I am gone from here."

PSALM 40

"I waited patiently for the Lord,
He inclined to me and heard my cry,
He brought me out of a horrible pit,
Put a song in my mouth and not a sigh.

Blessed is the man who makes the Lord his trust,
Many are the works Lord You have done,
Your thoughts towards us are so many,
They cannot be counted, not every one.

Sacrifices and burnt offerings You do not desire,
I said, "Behold I come it is written of Me,
I delight to do Your will O My God,
Your law in My heart will always be."

I have proclaimed the good news of righteousness,
My lips indeed I do not restrain,
O Lord You know I hide Your righteousness in my heart,
I declare Your faithful salvation again and again.

Be pleased O Lord to deliver me,
O Lord make haste to my helper be,
Let those who scoff at me be confounded,
May they be driven back and dishonor see.

Let those who seek You rejoice and be glad,
For when I am needy You think of me,
Let those who love You magnify Your name,

For You are my help and will always be."

PSALM 41

"Blessed is he who considers the poor,
All deliverance from trouble he will see,
The Lord will preserve him and keep him alive,
Strength on the bed of sickness his will be.

I said, 'Lord be merciful to me,
Heal me for I have sinned against You,'
My enemies ask, "When will his name perish?"
They speak only lies in all they do.

All who hate me whisper against me,
"An evil disease causes him to lie down," they say,
Even my friend who I really trusted is against me,
Though he ate bread with me many a day.

You O Lord be merciful to me,
Raise me up so them I can repay,
By this I will know that You are pleased,
For You have sent my enemy away.

As for me You uphold my integrity,
Set me before Your face again and again,
Blessed is the Lord God of Israel,
From everlasting to everlasting, Amen and Amen!"

BOOK 2

Psalms 42-72 v 20

PSALM 42

"As the deer pants for the brooks of water,
So my soul longs O God for You,
When shall I appear before the living God?
They say, "Where is you God?" yes many do.

My tears have been my food day and night,
While they continually say these words to me,
When I remember these sayings always,
The pouring out of my soul will be.

Why are you cast down O my soul?
Why be disquieted within me?
Hope in God for I shall yet praise Him,
For the help of His countenance will be.

O my God my soul is cast down,
From the Jordan I will remember You,
And also from the heights of Mount Herman,
And from the Hill Mizar too.

Deep calls to deep by the noise of Your waterfall,
All Your waves and billows have gone over me,
In the day the Lord commands His loving kindness,
In the night His song over me will be.

I will say to God my Rock,
'Why have You forgotten me?
Why do I go again mourning,

Because of the oppression of my enemy?'

Why are you cast down O my soul?
Why are you disquieted in me?
Hope in God for I will praise Him,
For the help of His countenance will be."

PSALM 43

"Vindicate me O God against an ungodly nation,
Deliver me from unjust and deceitful man,
You alone are the God of my strength,
Why do I mourn because of my enemy?
O Lord send Your light and truth as only You can.

Let Your light and truth lead me,
Let them bring to Your Holy Hill,
I will go to the altar of my God with joy,
Give Him praises on my harp I certainly will.

Why are you cast down O my soul?
Why are you disquieted in me?
I will hope and praise the Lord,
For He is my help and will always be."

PSALM 44

"We have heard with our ears O God,
Our fathers have told us all of Your deeds,
All of the deeds You did in their days,
How You provided all of their needs.

You drove out the nations before them,
Afflicting them and driving them out of the land,
For then our fathers were planted there,
By Your power and the strength of Your hand.

You are my King O God,
Victories for Jacob command You thus,
Through You we will defeat our enemies,
With Your name defeat all against us.

I will never trust in my bow,
Nor will my own sword save me,
You put to shame all those who hate us,
And again saved us from our enemy.

But then You cast us off in shame,
From the enemy You made us retreat,
You gave us like sheep for food,
Taking everything from under our feet.

You make us a reproach to our neighbours,
Those around us are filled with scorn,
My dishonor is always before me,

And shame as a covering by me is worn.

All this has come upon me,
But we have not forgotten You,
Nor have we broken Your command,
Following Your steps we always do.

If we had forgotten the name of our God,
On to foreign gods stretched out our hand,
Would not God know what is in our hearts,
And know how in statute we stand?

Would not God have searched this out?
Yet we are killed all the day long,
Yes we are counted as sheep for slaughter,
No strength when we once were strong.

Awake, why do you sleep O Lord?
Do not cast us off not ever,
Why hide Your face from our afflictions,
Leaving us down in the dust forever?

For our soul is indeed in the dust,
Our bodies cling again to the ground,
Redeem us for Your mercies sake,
For only in You is our help found."

PSALM 45

"My heart is overflowing with a good theme,
I recite my composition concerning the King,
My tongue is in the pen of the ready writer,
Praises from my heart I will sing.

You are fairer than the sons of men,
Grace poured upon your lips,
Therefore God has blessed you forever,
O mighty one gird your sword upon your hips.

With Your glory and Your majesty,
Ride prosperously with righteousness, truth and humility,
Your right hand teaches You awesome things,
Your arrows sharp in the hearts of Your enemy.

Your throne O God is forever and ever,
You love righteousness but the wicked You hate,
Anointed are You with the oil of gladness,
While kings daughters upon You wait.

Listen O daughter incline your ear,
Your father's house and own people forget,
So that the King will desire your beauty,
Worship Him, then the daughters of Tyre a gift for you will get.

The royal daughter is glorious in the palace,
In robes of gold and many colours, she is brought to the King,
The virgins, her companions shall be brought also,

With gladness and rejoicing, them they do bring."

PSALM 46

"God is our refuge and strength,
A present help in trouble is He,
Though the earth be removed we won't fear,
No, even when the mountains fall into the sea.

There is a river that makes God's City glad,
The Holy place, the Tabernacle of the Most High,
The nations rage and Kingdoms were moved,
Not the City, for God is her helper that's why.

The Lord of Hosts is with us,
The God of Jacob our refuge too,
Come behold the works of the Lord,
And all of His desolations view.

He breaks the bow and cuts the spear in two,
He makes wars to the ends of the earth cease,
He burns all the chariots with fire,
Then to the whole earth brings His peace.

"Be still and know that I am God,
Such a good thing for you to do!"
He will be exalted on earth and in nations,
The Lord of Hosts is always with you."

PSALM 47

"O clap your hands all you people,
A voice of triumph to God raise,
The Lord most high is awesome,
And deserves all of your praise.

He is King over all the earth,
He puts nations and people under our feet,
Because He loves the excellence of Jacob,
Our chosen inheritance will be complete.

God has gone up with a shout,
The Lord with the trumpet sound,
Sing praises to God our King, sing praises,
To the King of all the earth around.

God reigns over the nations from His Holy Throne,
Belonging to Him are all the earths shield,
The princes of the people are gathered together,
To the God of Abraham, they all will yield."

PSALM 48

"Great is the Lord and greatly to be praised,
His Holy mountain, beautiful in its height,
The joy of the whole earth is Mount Zion,
The city and palaces, the King's refuge filled with light.

The Kings assembled and passed by it,
They marveled but, being troubled hastened away,
Pain and fear as a woman in childbirth overtook them,
Like the ships of Tarshish in the strong winds sway.

We have thought O God on Your loving kindness,
In the midst of Your Temple, according to Your name,
So is Your praise and righteousness to the ends of the earth,
Let the daughters of Judah be glad for,
Your judgements are always the same.

Walk all around Zion, counting her towers bulwarks,
And palaces so to all generations you will confide,
For this is God, our God forever and ever,
He will unto death be our constant guide."

PSALM 49

"Hear this, peoples of the world and all inhabitants,
Both low and high, rich and poor, who together live,
My mouth shall speak wisdom and understanding,
That the meditation of my heart will give.

Why should I fear in the days of evil,
When the iniquity at my heels surrounds me?
Those who trust and boast in their riches,
Cannot even a redeemer of a brother be.

Nor give a ransom to God for him,
For the redemption of a soul costly is it,
He should continue to live forever,
And not see the inside of the pit.

The fool and the senseless person perish,
For he sees even wise men die,
They their wealth to others they leave,
'My house will live forever!' is their inner cry.

Their dwelling place give to all generations,
Calling their lands after their own name,
He is like the beasts who soon perishes,
But man though in honour does not remain.

This is the way of those who are foolish,
And their prosperity who approve all they say,
Like sheep they are laid in the grave,

And their beauty shall be consumed away.

The upright shall have dominion in the morning,
My God will not allow me to be in the grave laid,
For my God shall receive me forever,
To become rich will not make me afraid.

When the glory of his house is increased,
For when he dies he will carry nothing away,
His glory shall not descend after him,
Though he blesses himself every day.

He shall go to the generation of his fathers,
They shall never be in the light,
A man of honour yet does not understand,
Is like the beasts who perish at night."

PSALM 50

"The Mighty God the Lord has spoken and called the earth,
From the rising of the sun to its going down,
Our God shall come and not be silent,
With Him it shall be very tempestuous all around.

Out of Zion the beauty of God will shine forth,
He shall call, "Gather My saints together to Me."
This He calls to the heavens and to the earth,
And gathered together they will be.

"Those who have a covenant with Me by sacrifice,
Let His righteousness from heaven declared be,"
For God Himself is a righteous judge,
The truth of His judgement you will always see.

"Hear O My people and I will speak,
O Israel I will testify against you,
I am God your only true God,
I will not rebuke you for the sacrifices you do.

Your burnt offerings are always before Me,
I'll take not a bull from your house although it is fine,
For I own the cattle on a thousand hills,
And all the wild beasts of the field are mine."

The world is God's in all its fullness,
Pay your vows to the Most High,
Offer to God thanksgiving and praise,

He will deliver you and hear your cry.

"But to the wicked," God says,
"What right have you My statutes to declare,
Or take My covenant in your mouth,
Because for My instructions you do not care?

When you saw a thief you consented with him,
A partaker with adulterers you have been too,
Your mouth you give to evil slander,
And many things filled with deceit you do.

Lest I tear you in pieces, you who forget God,
Offer praises and glorify Me and do right,
Or there will be none to deliver you,
Then I will put the salvation of God in your sight."

PSALM 51

"Have mercy on me O God with tender mercy,
According to Your loving kindness begin,
Wash me from my iniquity and transgressions,
Cleanse me from all of my sin.

I acknowledge my sin and transgressions,
For they are always there before me,
Against You and only against You have I sinned,
Knowing that my actions You would see.

Behold I was brought forth in iniquity,
In sin my mother conceived me,
You desire truth in the hidden parts,
In the hidden parts Your wisdom I will see.

Purge me with hyssop and I shall be clean,
Wash me and I shall be whiter than snow,
Fill me with joy and gladness,
Hide Your face and my sins will all go.

Create in me a clean heart O God,
A steadfast spirit in me renew,
Do not cast me from Your presence,
Taking Your Holy Spirit from me please don't do.

Restore to me the joy of Your salvation,
By Your generous Spirit me always uphold,
Then I will teach all transgressors Your ways,

They will obey everything that to them I have told.

Deliver me from the guilt of bloodshed,
O God of my salvation now hear me,
My tongue will sing loudly of Your righteousness,
No more shall Your desire for sacrifice be.

You do not desire burnt offerings,
But a broken and contrite heart,
These O God You will not despise,
When these I give to You we will never part.

Do good in Your good pleasure to Zion,
Build again the walls of Jerusalem,
With sacrifices of righteousness you will be pleased,
Burnt offerings and bulls receive them."

PSALM 52

"Why do you boast in evil O mighty man?
Your tongue like a sharp razor working deceit,
Why do you love evil more than good?
Lies from your tongue you always speak.

God shall likewise destroy you forever,
From your dwelling place pluck you away,
Because you strengthen yourself in wickedness,
He will uproot you from the living one day.

The righteous shall see this and fear,
And shall laugh at the man and say,
He trusted in the abundance of his riches,
He did not trust God and went his own way.

But I am like a green olive tree in the house of God,
I trust in the mercy of God forever and ever,
I will praise You forever for what You have done,
I will wait on Your good name, leaving it never."

PSALM 53

"The fool has said in his heart, "There is no God,"
They are corrupt and filled with iniquity,
Ever one has turned aside,
There is none who do good that You could see.

Have the workers of iniquity no knowledge,
Who eat up My people as they eat bread?
There is great fear where no fear was,
They do not call upon God instead.

God has scattered the bones of your enemy,
The one who encamps against you,
You have managed to put them to shame,
Because God has despised them too.

Oh that salvation should come out of Zion,
When God His captive people bring back,
Let Jacob rejoice and Israel be glad,
For God's people are no more in lack."

PSALM 54

"Save me O God by Your name,
By Your strength vindicate me,
Give ear O God to my words and prayer,
For those against me strangers be.

Those strangers have risen up against me,
And oppressors seek after my life,
They have not set God before them,
For they are people of strife.

Behold God is my helper,
The Lord is with those who my life uphold,
My enemies He their evil will repay,
Cut them off with Your truth that's told.

I will freely sacrifice to You,
I will always praise Your name,
O Lord for Your name is good,
And forever the same.

The Lord has delivered me out of trouble,
Set me free from my enemies,
And my eyes have seen it all,
For the desires of my eyes I see."

PSALM 55

"Give ear to my prayer O God,
Do not from my supplication hide,
I noisily moan and complain, attend and hear me,
I am restless because of my enemy's voice,
Trouble and hatred from them will be.

My heart is severely pained within me,
And the terrors of death I surely see,
Fearfulness and trembling upon me have come,
And horror has overwhelmed me.

'O,' said I, 'If only I had wings like a dove,'
I could fly and wander in the wilderness,
I would fly away to the sky up above,
And escape from the storm and tempest.

Destroy O Lord and divide their tongues,
For I have seen violence and strife in the city,
Day and night they go around its walls,
In the midst of it is trouble and iniquity.

Oppression and deceit do not part,
Destruction is in the midst of the city,
It is not an enemy who reproaches me,
But a friend who shows me no pity.

If it was one who hated me I would hide,
But it was one who was equal to me,

My companion and acquaintance,
In sweet counsel together were we.

Let death surely seize them all,
Or let them alive go down to hell,
For wickedness is in their dwellings,
And amongst them all as well.

As for me I will call upon God,
And the Lord will set me free,
I will pray and cry aloud,
For there are many against me.

God will hear and afflict them,
Even He who abides from of old,
Because they never do change,
Fear not God and are so bold.

He has put forth his hands against his friends,
All those who with him were at peace,
His words were smooth and soft like butter and oil,
And his promises he did cease.

Cast your burden upon the Lord,
Moving the righteous He will not permit,
He will forever sustain you,
And send the wicked down in the pit."

PSALM 56

"Be merciful to me O God lest man swallow me up,
By fighting all day he oppresses me,
My enemies hound me all day long,
Many O God fighting against me will be.

Whenever I am afraid I will trust in You,
I will praise and in You God I will trust,
Because of You I will not fear flesh,
What can they do to me, for lean on God I must.

All day long they twist my words,
For evil are their thoughts against me,
Together they hide and mark my steps,
They want to take my life, will they escape by iniquity?

You O Lord number my wanderings,
In a bottle You put all my tears,
Are they not all in Your book,
When I cry to You about all of my fears?

Then my enemies will turn back,
This I know for God is for me,
I will always praise the Word of God,
Having no fear for in God my trust will be.

Vows to You are binding to me O God,
I will render my praise to You ,
For You have delivered my soul from death,

Walking before God in the light of the living I do."

PSALM 57

"Be merciful to me O God,
Be merciful for I trust in You,
In the shadow of Your wings I am safe,
Until calamities pass by as they will do.

I will cry out to God Most High,
To God who performs all things for me,
He reproaches the one who would swallow me up,
My salvation from heaven will be.

Be exalted O God above the heavens,
Let Your glory be above all the earth,
My soul is so bowed down,
Yet I will praise You with all my worth.

My enemies have prepared a net for me,
Before me they have dug a pit,
They thought to catch me in pit and net,
But they have fallen themselves into it.

My heart is steadfast O God,
I will sing and give praise to You,
I will sing to You amongst the nations,
For Your love and mercy are so true.

Be exalted O God above the heavens,
Let Your glory be above all the earth,
For I will sing praises O God,

And worship You for all Your worth."

PSALM 58

"Do you speak righteousness you silent ones?
Upright in judgement do you maintain?
No, in your hearts is wickedness and violence,
Which you in the earth, you weigh out again and again.

The wicked are estranged from the womb,
Lying as soon as they are born, go astray,
They are like the deaf cobra whose ear is stopped,
Which cannot hear the skillful charmer's way.

Break their teeth in their mouth O God,
Break the fangs of young lions too,
O Lord let them like continuous waters flow,
And as stillborn seeing the sun they cannot do.

God shall take them away as with a whirlwind,
As His living and burning wrath He shows,
How He wreaks His judgement on the earth,
If there is a reward for the righteous God Himself knows."

PSALM 59

"Deliver me from my enemies O God,
Defend me from those rising up against me,
And save me from the bloodthirsty men,
Deliver me from the workers of iniquity,
They look and they lay in wait for my life.

The mighty are gathered against me,
Not for my sins or transgressions O Lord,
Do they run and prepare,
So my fault it cannot be.

Awake to help me and behold O Lord,
Lord God of Hosts and Israel are You,
Awake to punish all of the nations,
Showing mercy to the wicked You do not do.

At evening growling like dogs they return,
Going around the city belching away,
Their words are like swords on their lips,
For, "Who can hear us?" they say.

But You O Lord shall laugh at them,
You shall hold all nations in derision,
I will wait, for my God of mercy will come to meet me,
And I will see my desire for my enemies in a vison.

Do not slay them lest My people forget no scatter them,
By Your power and bring them down O Lord our shield,

Take them for their pride their lying and cursing,
O Lord upon them Your wrath wield.

At the evening, growling like dogs they return,
Consume them as unsatisfied, they wander looking for food,
Let them know that God over Jacob rules and also,
Ruling over the whole earth to the end, showing good.

But I will sing of Your power O God,
Of Your mercy in the morning I will sing,
For You are my refuge and defense,
For Your mercy and strength, praise I will bring."

PSALM 60

"O God You have cast us off and broken us down,
You make the earth tremble for You are displeased,
Heal the earth for You have shaken it,
It trembles because it is surely breached.

You have made us drink the wine of confusion,
And show Your people many a hard thing,
Restore us O Lord, restore us again,
So we may rejoice in the peace that will bring.

You have given a banner to those who fear You,
That because of its truth they may display,
Then Your beloved will be delivered,
With Your right hand Lord save the day.

God has spoken in His holiness,
"I will rejoice and divide Shechem in two,
Gilead is Mine, Manasseh is Mine,
I will measure the valley of Succoth too.

Ephraim is a helmet for My head,
And Judah is My lawgiver too,
Moab will be to Me a wash pot,
Over Edom I will cast My shoe.

Philistia will shout in triumph because of Me,"
Who will bring me to the strong city?
Who will again lead me to Edom?

You who cast us off please take pity.

And You O God who did not join our armies,
Help us O Lord in our troubles hear our pleas,
In God we will do valiantly, man is useless,
It is God who will tread down our enemies."

PSALM 61

"Hear O God my cry attend to my prayer,
From the end of the earth I cry to you,
When my heart is sorely overwhelmed,
Lead me to the rock that is higher, please do.

For You have been a shelter for me,
A strong tower from the enemy,
I will abide in Your Tabernacle forever,
Under the shelter of Your wing my trust will be.

For You O God have heard my vows,
The heritage of those who fear is given to me,
You will prolong the king's life and preserve him,
And his years many generations shall be.

I shall abide forever before God,
For mercy and truth I will praise Your name,
I will sing praises to You forever,
Then I will perform my vows again."

PSALM 62

"Truly my soul silently waits for God,
He alone is my rock of salvation,
From Him is my salvation and defense,
Which I shall not be moved from in this nation.

How long will you be attacking a man?
Like leaning walls and tottering fences are slain,
They do consult to cast me from my position,
Cursing inwardly they bless with their mouth again.

My soul waits silently for God alone,
He is my rock of salvation I have proved,
My expectation is only from Him,
He is my defense and I shall not be moved.

Trust in Him at all times you people,
Before Him pour out your heart,
For He is our refuge and strength,
So give Him your heart, make a start.

Surely men of low degree are but a vapour
And those of high degree are a lie,
They are altogether lighter than vapour,
So their weight is low but their degree is high.

Do not trust in robbery,
And not in oppression too,
Do not set your heart on riches,

For they will not do good for you.

God has spoken once,
Twice I have heard this,
That power and mercy belong to God,
According to each ones work He gives them this."

PSALM 63

"O God You are my God, early I will seek You,
My soul thirsts and longs for You, my flesh longs for You too,
In a dry and thirsty land where all the water is gone,
I have looked for You in the Sanctuary,
Where Your power and glory have shone.

Because Your loving kindness is better than life,
My lips shall praise and bless while I live,
I will lift up my hands in Your name,
My mouth with joyful lips praise to You will give.

When I remember You on my bed,
I meditate in the watches at night,
Because You are my help, in Your wings shadow I rejoice,
And Your right hand helps me to walk in the light.

But those who seek my life to destroy it,
Shall go into the lower parts of the earth,
Then shall everyone fall by the sword,
To a portion of jackals is all they are worth.

But the King shall in God rejoice,
All who swear by Him shall glory,
Those who tell lies shall have their mouth stopped,
So they cannot tell another story."

PSALM 64

"Hear my voice O God in my meditation,
Preserve my life from my enemy,
Hide me from the secret plots of the wicked,
From rebellious workers of iniquity.

Who sharpen their tongues like swords,
And bend their bows to shoot,
Bitter words like arrows in their bows,
Their hatred of the blameless is their causes root.

They encourage themselves in an evil matter,
Talk in secret of laying a snare,
They say that none will see them,
Or of their iniquities become aware.

Both the thoughts and heart of a man are deep,
As they perfect so shrewd a scheme,
But God shall shoot them with an arrow,
So that wounded they will flee the scene.

Then God will make their tongues stumble,
All who see them shall flee away,
Men shall fear and declare the works of God,
And shall wisely consider God's way.

While they think about what God is doing,
The righteous in God shall be glad,
The upright will always trust in Him,

Knowing there is no glory in being bad."

PSALM 65

"Praise is awaiting O God is Zion,
A vow will be performed for You,
Iniquities and transgressions prevail against me,
Atonement for them all You provide too.

Blessed is the man You choose,
The one You call to approach You,
To dwell in Your courts to the satisfaction of goodness,
In Your house and Holy Temple too.

By awesome deeds in righteousness You will answer us,
The God of our salvation answers all our needs,
You are the confidence of the whole earth,
You establish the mountains and far off seas.

By the power of Your strength O God,
You still the noise of the waves in the seas,
Those who live in the farthest parts fear these signs,
When the morning and evening outgoings rejoice, they are pleased.

You visit the earth and water it,
Your river O God overflows,
You provide water for their grain,
You settle its ridges and furrows.

You make the earth soft with showers,
The little hills on every side rejoice,
The pastures are covered with flocks,

The valleys covered with grain,
They sing and shout with a loud voice."

PSALM 66

"Make a joyful shout to God all the earth,
Sing out the honour of His name,
Make His praise glorious,
Say to God, 'How awesome are Your works!' it is plain.

Through the greatness of Your power,
Your enemies submit themselves to You,
All the earth shall worship and sing praises,
Sing praises to Your name they will do.

Come and see the awesome works of God,
Into dry land He turned the sea,
All the people crossed the river on foot,
Rejoicing forever in God's power they will be.

O bless our God you peoples,
And make His praise to be heard,
Who keeps our souls among the living,
And holds us up by His word.

You do not allow our feet to be moved,
You O God have put us through the test,
Refined as silver we went through fire and water,
But our fulfilment was of the very best.

I will go into Your house with burnt offerings,
I will pay my vows for my lips have uttered that,
I will offer burnt sacrifices of animals,

A sweet aroma of bulls and goats burning fat.

Come and hear all those who fear God,
I will declare what He has for my every part,
With my mouth I cried unto Him,
In case I regard iniquity in my heart.

Certainly God always hears me,
He attends to the sound of my voice,
Blessed be God He does not turn away,
For His mercy I will always rejoice."

PSALM 67

"God be merciful to us and bless us,
Cause Your face on us to shine,
That You may always be known on earth,
Your salvation on all nations is divine.

Let the people always praise You,
O God let all the people praise You,
Then the earth will yield increase,
For judging them is what You do.

You govern the nations O Lord,
Let the people all praise You,
Then the earth will yield this increase,
Blessing Your people You surely do.

God, our own God will bless us,
And all the ends of the earth shall fear,
Let all the people praise the Lord,
That He will bless us is so clear."

PSALM 68

"Let God arise and His enemies be scattered,
Let those who hate before Him flee,
As smoke is driven away drive them,
As wax melts in a fire they will be.

So let the wicked perish at God's presence,
But let the righteous be exceedingly glad,
Let them all rejoice before God,
For all the good things they have had.

Sing to God sing praises to His name,
Extol Him who rides on a cloud,
By His name YAH rejoice before Him,
Rejoice with praises sing for Him aloud.

A Father of the fatherless is He,
A defender of widows too,
And God in His Holy Habitation,
If you are lonely He takes care of you.

O God when You went out before Your people,
When You marched in the wilderness,
At Your presence the earth shook,
You with rain the earth did bless.

Yes O God You sent plentiful rain,
Confirmed the inheritance belonging to You,
Your weary congregation dwelt in it O God,

In Your goodness that You provide for the poor is true.

The Lord gave the word,
A great company declared it,
Kings of the armies did flee, yes they flee,
She who stays at home will divide the spoil,
A good sharer of the spoil she will be.

Though you lie down among the sheepfold,
You will be covered by silver, like the wings of a dove,
Her feathers are gold, and God scatters kings in it,
As Zalmon is white, covered in snow from above.

The mountain of God is the mountain of Bashan,
A mountain of many peaks is Bashan,
Do not envy you many peaked mountains,
For this is the mountain God desires to dwell in,
You must understand.

The chariots of God are thousands of thousands,
The Lord is among them as in Sinai the Holy place,
You O Lord have led captivity captive,
You have ascended on high full of grace.

Blessed be the Lord for all His benefits,
The God of our salvation is He,
Unto Him belong escapes from death,
From Him our deliverance will be.

For God will wound the head of His enemy,
The hairy scalp of one whose trespasses we see,
The Lord said, "I will bring back from Bashan,
I will bring back from the depths of the sea."

They have seen Your procession O God,
Which into the sanctuary goes my Lord and King,
The players of instruments and maidens and timbrels,
Praising and blessing God, the congregation sing.

Your God has commanded your strength,
Strengthen all of us O God as You do,
Because of Your temple, all Jerusalem,
And kings will bring presents to You.

Sing to God you kingdoms of the earth,
Sing praises to the Lord, sing praises to the Lord,
For the God of Israel gives strength to His people,
So sing and praise with joy all in one accord."

PSALM 69

"Save me O God my God,
For waters are up to my neck,
And I am in the deep mire,
I have come into deep waters,
To be free and standing is my desire.

Where the floods overflow me,
I am weary with my cry,
My eyes fail while I wait for God,
My throat has become so dry.

Those who hate me without a cause,
Are more than the hairs on my head,
They are mighty who would destroy me,
I cry to You O God at night in my bed.

O God You know my foolishness,
And my sins are not hidden from You,
Let those who wait for You O God,
Be ashamed of me and those who seek,
Not be confounded too.

Because for your sake I have borne reproach,
I have become a stranger to my brother,
Because zeal for your house has eaten me up,
I am alien to the children of my mother.

When I wept and chastened myself with fasting,

The reproach of those who reproach You is on me,
I also made my garments as sackcloth,
The reproach of the drunkard I shall be.

As for me my prayer is to You,
O Lord in the acceptable time,
O God in the multitude of You mercy,
Hear me and let the truth of salvation be mine.

Let me be delivered out of the mire,
And delivered from those who hate me,
Let not the deep swallow me up,
May I out of the deep waters be.

Hear me O Lord for Your loving kindness,
Your loving kindness is always good,
Turn to me according to Your tender mercy,
Praise You for my deliverance I should.

You know my reproach, my dishonor,
My adversaries are all before You,
Let their table become a snare,
Let their wellbeing be a trap too.

Let also their eyes be darkened,
So that they no longer can see,
Pour out Your indignation before them,
Let their dwelling also desolate be.

But I am poor and so sorrowful,
Let Your salvation set me on high,
I will magnify You with thanksgiving,
For You always answer my cry.

This also shall please the Lord,
Better than an ox or a bull,
The humble shall see and be glad,
The poor live with hearts that are full.

Let heaven and earth praise the Lord,
And everything that moves in the seas,
God will save Zion and build Judah,
So all that love His name live in peace."

PSALM 70

"Make haste O God, make haste to deliver me,
Let them be confounded who seek my life,
Let them be turned back and confused,
Let them be ashamed of their strife.

Let those who seek You rejoice,
Let them also be glad in You,
And those who love Your salvation say,
"Let God be magnified for all he does do!"

But I am poor and needy,
O God make haste to me today,
You are my help, my deliverer,
O Lord make haste do not delay."

PSALM 71

"In You O Lord do I put my trust,
Let me never be put to shame,
Deliver me in Your righteousness,
Incline Your ear and save me again.

Deliver me O God out of the hand of the wicked,
Out of the hand of the unrighteous and cruel man,
For You are my hope O Lord my God,
Forever I will praise, for in You I stand.

I have become a wonder to many,
My praise for You and Your glory is every day,
You O Lord are my strong refuge,
My praise for You will never delay.

Do not cast me off at the time of old age,
Do not forsake when strength fails me,
Those who lie in wait for my life take counsel,
And my enemies speaking against me will be.

O God do not be far from me,
O my God make haste to help me,
Let the enemies of my life be confounded,
And my adversaries all consumed be.

I will always hope and praise You,
Yes, more and more praise You,
My mouth shall tell of Your righteousness,

And speak of all the good things You do.

O God You have taught me since my youth,
And when I am old and my head grey,
I will go in the strength of the Lord,
Making mention of Your righteousness very day.

You have done such great things,
O God there is none like You,
You have shown me many troubles,
But bringing me out of them too.

O Lord with the lute I will praise You,
I will sing with the harp to You,
My lips shall greatly rejoice O God,
When all Your great goodness I view."

PSALM 72

"Give the king Your judgement O God,
And Your righteousness to the king's son,
He will judge Your people righteously,
Justice to the poor will be done.

The mountains bring peace to the people,
The little hills by righteousness do,
He will save the children of the needy,
Break in pieces the oppressors too.

As long as the sun and the moon endure,
They shall continue to fear You,
Throughout all of the nations,
Coming down like rain He will do.

Like showers that water the earth,
The righteous shall flourished be,
An abundance of peace 'til the moon is gone,
And He shall have dominion over the sea.

From the river to the ends of the earth,
In the wilderness those who dwell there will bow,
The kings of Tarshish shall bring presents,
All the kings before Him fall down now.

He will deliver the needy when they cry,
The poor and those without helpers too,
He will indeed save the poor and needy,

Precious shall be their blood in His view.

His name shall endure forever,
His name continue as long as the sun,
All men shall be blessed by Him,
Blessed shall He be by nations every one!

Blessed be the Lord God of Israel,
Who does many wonderful things and then,
Blessed be His glorious name forever,
Let the whole earth be filled with His Glory,
AMEN and AMEN!!!

BOOK 3

Psalms 73-89 v 52

PSALM 73

"Truly God is good to Israel,
To such as are the poor of heart,
As for me I nearly slipped and stumbled,
For I envied the boastful their prosperous part.

When I saw the prosperity of the wicked,
They are not in troubles like other men,
They wear pride on their necks like necklaces,
And a garment of violence covers them.

Their eyes bulge for their abundance,
They have more than the wishes of their heart,
They speak loftily, set their mouth against the heavens,
Their tongue walks over the earth every part.

Therefore his people return here,
The full cup of water by them drained dry,
They say, "How does God know all these things?
For is all knowledge in the Most High?"

Behold the ungodly is increased in riches,
Who are always at their ease,
Surely my heart is cleansed in vain,
For all day long I am plagued,
Not even in the morning does it cease.

Behold I would have been untrue to Your children's generation,
If I had spoken without understanding too,

All of this was so painful to me,
Then into the sanctuary I went,
And got O God, a good understanding from You.

I found You had set them in slippery places,
They are full of terror, a bad dream is all it takes,
O how they are brought down in desolation,
You will Lord, despise their image when You awake.

Thus my heart was utterly grieved,
And I so vexed in my mind,
I was so foolish and ignorant,
Yet You are always with me I find.

You hold me by Your right hand,
I will always be guided by You,
Only You, do I have in heaven,
Receive me into Your glory O God, do.

There is none upon earth that I desire,
For God You are the strength of my heart,
I have put my trust in You Lord God,
To declare Your works I will start."

PSALM 74

"O God why have You cast us off forever?
Why does Your anger smoke against Your sheep?
Remember Your congregation purchased of old,
And the tribe of Your inheritance that You keep.

Lift up Your feet to perpetual desolation,
The enemy has completely damaged the sanctuary,
Your enemies roar in the middle of Your meeting places,
Lifting up banners for signs they will be.

They break down with axes and hammers carved work,
They have defiled the place of Your name to the ground,
In their hearts they say, "Let us destroy them altogether!"
Burning up all the places of God to be found.

We have no signs, there are no longer prophets,
O God how long will the reproach of the adversary be?
Will the enemy blaspheme Your name forever?
The destruction by Your right hand we will see.

For God is my King from of old,
Working salvation in the earth for our good,
You divided the sea with Your strength,
Filled those in the wilderness with Leviathan food.

You broke open the fountain and the flood,
Belonging to You is the day and the night,
You have set all the borders of the earth,

You have prepared the sun giving light.

Remember this, the enemy has reproached O Lord,
And foolish people have blasphemed Your name,
O do not forget Your poor people forever,
You covenant us all not to see shame.

Arise O God plead Your own cause,
O do not let the oppressed see shame,
Remember the foolish reproach You daily,
But let the poor and needy praise Your name."

PSALM 75

"We give thanks to you O God, give thanks,
Your wondrous works declare Your name,
"In the proper time I will judge uprightly,
And put those who boast to shame."

For exaltation does not come from the east,
Nor from the south or the west,
For God is judge, He will put one down,
And another He exalts as the best.

For in the hand of the Lord is a cup,
Fully mixed He pours wine that is red,
Surely the wicked will drink it down,
And drain the cup to the last dreg.

But I will declare O God forever,
My praise to the God of Jacob will be,
"The strength of the righteous shall be exalted,
The strength of the wicked cut off by Me!"

PSALM 76

"In Judah God's name is well known,
In Zion He broke the arrows and bow,
In Israel they hold God up as great,
As the Tabernacle and Salem do know.

You are more glorious and excellent O God,
Than all the mountains of prey,
The stout hearted were plundered and sleep,
How to use their hands, the mighty have not found a way.

At Your rebuke O God of Jacob,
Both chariot and horse fall into the sleep of the dead,
You O Lord are much to be feared,
None can stand, because of Your anger they are filled with dread.

You have caused judgement to be heard from heaven,
The earth feared and was very still,
When God arose to deliver judgement,
Surely the wrath of man shall praise You at will.

Make vows and pay them to the Lord your God,
Let all who fear Him bring presents too,
He shall cut off the spirit of princes,
To the kings of the earth, He is awesome,
All of them, not just a few."

PSALM 77

"I cried out to God with my voice,
And He gave ear unto me,
In my day of trouble, I cried to the Lord,
I cried, 'O Lord let me my answer see.'

My hand stretched out in the night,
My soul comforted would not be,
I remembered God and was troubled,
My spirit was overwhelmed in me.

You hold my eyelids open,
I am troubled and cannot speak,
I have considered ancient days of old,
Remembrance of them all I seek.

Will the Lord cast off forever?
Has His promise forever more failed?
Has God forgotten to be gracious,
Or is He angry because I have wailed?

This then is my anguish,
As I remember the years,
Of the right hand of the Most High,
When He delivered me from all my fears.

I will remember the works of the Lord,
Surly I will remember wonders of old,
I will meditate on all of Your work,

Your ways O God in the sanctuary I behold.

Who is as great as our God?
You do many wonders every day,
You have with Your arm redeemed,
Your strength to Jacob and Joseph You display.

The waters saw You and were afraid,
Clouds poured their water, depths trembled too,
Your thunder was in the whirlwind,
O God what more showing of power will You do?

The lightening lit up the world,
The whole earth trembled and shook,
You led Your people like a flock,
Moses and Aaron wrote it all in The Book!"

PSALM 78

"Give ear O My people to My law,
Listen to the word I speak to you,
I will open my mouth in a parable,
Utter dark sayings of old I will do.

The ones which we have heard O God,
The ones our fathers to us made known,
We will not hide them from our children,
To all generations Your parables are shown.

All generations come to praise the Lord,
For the wonderful works He has done,
He established a testimony in Jacob,
Which He commanded our fathers, every one.

That they might let them be known to the children,
To all the children that are born,
That they will set their hope in God,
And garments of praise shall be worn.

That they will obey God's commandments,
So like their fathers they will not be,
They were a stubborn and rebellious nation,
Whose spirit did not follow God faithfully.

Marvelous things God did before their fathers,
He made waters in a heap stand,
He divided the sea and they all passed through,

Arriving safely back on dry land.

He split the rocks in the wilderness,
To give them pure water to drink,
He also made streams out of the rocks,
How to survive, they did not have to think.

But they sinned even more against God,
By asking now for more fancy food,
Therefore, the Lord heard and was furious,
Because they did not think His salvation was good.

Yet He had commanded the heavens above,
And of heaven He had opened the door,
He rained down manna for them to eat,
After this He did so much more.

He also rained down meat from heaven,
Feathered fowl, like sand of the sea,
He let them fall in the midst of the camp,
So that the people full and satisfied would be.

For He gave them their own desire,
Everything that they did crave,
But the wrath of God came upon them,
Many were struck dead and went in the grave.

When He slew them, they then sought Him,
They returned and sought God earnestly,
Then they remembered God was their rock,
The Most High their redeemer would be.

But how often they provoked Him in the wilderness,
And grieved Him so much in the desert too,
They limited the Holy One of Israel,
He could not do all the good He wanted to do.

They did not remember His power,
Or the signs in Egypt through Moses He did do,

He turned Egypt's rivers into blood,
Made all the streams flow with blood too.

He sent swarms of flies to devour,
Frogs and caterpillars ate every crop,
The rest was eaten by locusts,
Only Moses could make it stop.

He destroyed the firstborn of Egypt,
But His own people went forth like sheep,
He brought them to His Holy border,
And gave them good land to keep.
Moreover God rejected the tent of Jacob,
Nor did He choose Ephraim's tribe,
He chose Zion and the tribe of Judah,
Then in His sanctuary He chose to abide.

He also chose His servant David,
From the ewes and sheepfold to part,
For God knew He would shepherd His people,
For he was a man after God's own heart."

PSALM 79

"O God, nations have Your inheritance,
Your Temple defiled, Jerusalem in a heap,
The dead of Your saints given for bird food,
No one to bury them, none to mourn or to weep.

How long Lord will You be angry forever?
Will Your jealousy burn like fire?
Pour out Your wrath on those who don't know You,
Your deliverance of us all is our desire.

Oh do not remember iniquities against us,
Let Your mercies come to us with speed,
For we have been brought so very low,
Your salvation O God is all that we need.

For the glory of Your name deliver us,
Deliver and provide atonement for our sin,
Why should the nations cry, 'Where is their God?'
The avenging of Your servants blood we want to win.

Let the groaning of those in prison come before You,
According to the greatness of Your name O Lord,
Preserve all those appointed to die with nothing,
Return all to them sevenfold with Your word."

PSALM 80

"Give ear O Shepherd of Israel,
Joseph like a flock You lead,
You who dwell between the Cherubim,
Shine forth as to You we heed.

Before Abraham, Ephraim and Benjamin,
Restore O God make Your face to shine,
Stir up Your strength to save us all,
Our salvation O God will be fine.

O God how long will You be angry?
Your people pray long with tears,
You have made us a strife to our neighbours,
Restore O Lord and take away our fears.

You have brought a vine from Egypt,
You have prepared room for it,
And caused it to take deep root,
It has filled the land every bit.

The hills were covered with its shadow,
And the mighty cedars covered too,
She sent out her branches to the sea,
Sent her branches to the rivers she did do.

Why have You broken down her hedges,
So all pick her fruit as they pass by?
The boar of the woods uproots it,

And wild beasts devour it, O why?

Return we beseech You O God of hosts,
Look down from heaven and see,
Visit the vine and the vineyard You planted,
You made it as strong as can be.

But it is burned with fire, it is cut down,
They perish at the rebuke in Your face,
Put Your hand on Your right hand man,
Then we will be saved once again."

PSALM 81

"Sing aloud to God our strength,
Join in all you people take part,
To the God of Jacob joyfully shout,
Raise a song, play timbrel lute and harp.

Blow the trumpet at the new moon time,
At the full moon on our solemn feast day,
This is the law of the God of Jacob,
Let all praise Him and be swift to obey.

He established the testimony of Joseph,
When he went through all Egypt's land,
There are all God's statutes for Israel,
And I heard a language I did not understand.

"Hear O My people and I will admonish,
O Israel, if only You would listen to Me,
There shall be no foreign god among you,
I am your Lord God and always will be.

Yes I am the God who delivered you,
From the land of Egypt and slavery,
Open your mouth wide and I will fill it,
You will worship again only Me!

But My people would not hear My voice,
And Israel would have none of Me,
I gave them over to their stubborn hearts,

143

Walking in their own counsel they will be.

O that My people would listen to Me,
That Israel would walk in My way,
I would soon subdue their enemies,
And turn their adversaries away.

Those who hate the Lord pretend to submit,
But forever will be their fate,
I would have fed them the finest wheat,
And put honey from the rock on their plate."

PSALM 82

"God stands in the congregation of the mighty,
And amongst the mighty judges,
Says God, "How long will you judge unjustly?
With partiality to the wicked you are shod!

Defend the poor and fatherless,
Do justice to the afflicted and those in need,
Deliver all the poor and needy,
As from the wicked they are freed.

I have said, 'Yes you are gods,'
All are children of the Most High,
But you shall die like men and princes,
This you do not know or understand why."

Arise O God to inherit all nations,
For You O God shall their judge be,
All the foundations of the earth now are unstable,
And their salvation they need to see."

PSALM 83

"Do not be silent O God,
Do not forever hold Your peace,
For behold Your enemies make a tumult,
O God do not be still and at ease.

Those who hate you have lifted their head,
They have taken crafty counsel,
Against the people belonging to You,
Consulted together against Your sheltered ones,
Making wicked plans is what they do.

They consult together with one consent,
They form a confederacy against You,
They say, "Let us cut them off as a nation,
That the name of Israel is no longer in view."

Deal with them as Sisera and Midian,
As with Jabin at the Brook Kishon,
"So let us take all for our possession,
So make the pastures of God to us belong."

O God make them like the whirlwind,
Like chaff before the wind is dust,
As the fire that burns in the woods,
Pursue them with Your tempest You must.
Frighten them with Your storm,
O God fill their faces with shame,
Let them be confounded forever,

That they may seek Your name.

You let them be put to shame and perish,
That they know You, for Lord is Your name,
For You are the Most high forever,
And this knowledge will always be the same."

PSALM 84

"How lovely is your tabernacle O Lord of Hosts,
My soul longs for the courts of God alone,
My heart and flesh cry out for the living God,
For even a sparrow has found a good home.

And the swallow finds a nest for herself,
Where she may lay her young in the very best,
Even at Your altars O Lord of Hosts,
Those who dwell in Your house are blessed.

As they pass through the valley of Baca,
From strength to strength they go,
Each one appears before God in Zion,
Your glory O God they now know.

O Lord God of Hosts hear my prayer,
Give ear O God of Jacob to my plea,
And look upon the face of Your anointed,
And our shield You will surely be.

For a day in Your courts is a thousand,
A doorkeeper in God's house I would rather be,
Than to dwell in the tents of the wicked,
For our Lord God is a shield for me.

For the Lord God is a sun and shield,
The Lord gives glory and grace,
He withholds nothing from the upright,

Who keeps his faith in God in place."

PSALM 85

"Lord You have brought back the captivity of Jacob,
And have given favour to Your land,
You have forgiven the iniquities of Your people,
And covered their sin with Your right hand.

Yes You have covered their sin,
And taken away all Your wrath,
You have turned from Your fierce anger,
And put Your people on the straight path.

Restore O God of our salvation,
And cause Your anger towards us to cease,
Will You be angry forevermore?
Will You not revive us and give us Your peace?

Will Your anger last to all generations?
Will You never revive and blot out sins stain,
That Your people may rejoice in You?
Show Your mercy O Lord to us again.

I will hear what the Lord God will speak,
For to His people and saints He speaks peace,
Surely His salvation is near those who fear Him,
Let them not turn back and let their folly cease.

That glory may dwell in our land,
Mercy and truth together have met,
Righteousness and peace have now kissed,

God's truth springing out the earth will get.

And righteousness shall look down from heaven,
Yes the Lord will give all that is good,
Our Lord will yield to the earth its increase,
Righteousness will go before Him as it should."

PSALM 86

"Bow down Your ear O Lord and hear me,
Preserve my life for poor and needy am I,
I am holy for You are my God,
Be merciful to me O Lord I cry.

Rejoice O Lord the soul of Your servant,
For O Lord I lift up my soul to You,
For You O Lord are ready to forgive,
Showing mercy to those who call is what You do.

Among the gods there is none like You,
For all the nations You have made too,
Shall come before You and worship You,
For the wondrous things You do.

Teach me Your way O Lord,
Unite my heart to fear Your name,
I will praise You O Lord my God,
Heart and soul Yours, I will always remain.

For great is Your mercy towards me,
From the depths of Sheol You rescued me,
I will glorify Your name forever,
For truth You have always helped me to see.

O God the proud have risen against me,
A mob of violent men seek my life,
I have not set You before them,

For they are wicked and full of strife.

But You O Lord are a God of compassion,
Long suffering and abundant in mercy and grace,
O turn to me and have mercy,
I need Your mercy and truth in this place.

Give Your strength to Your servant,
Show me a sign for good O Lord,
Let those who hate me be ashamed,
When they see my salvation by Your word."

PSALM 87

"The Lord loves the gates of Zion,
Glorious things are spoken of You,
Your foundations are in the Holy mountains,
The dwellings of Jacob You love too.

Behold Philistia, Tyre and Babylon,
I will make mention of those who know me,
I will make mention of Rahab in Babylon,
This one was born there you see.

This one and that one was born is Zion,
She will be established by the Most High,
The Lord will record where He registers the people,
This one was born there is the reason why."

PSALM 88

"O Lord God of my salvation,
Day and night before you I cry,
Incline Your ear, let my cry come before You,
My soul full of troubles makes me sigh.

And my life draws near to the grave,
I am counted with those who go to the pit,
I am like a man who has no strength,
Adrift like the dead and a grave with stains in it.

Like the slain who lie in the grave,
Cut off by Your hand remembered no more,
You have laid me in the lowest pit,
In the darkest depths no more to implore.

You have afflicted me with all Your waves,
You have put my acquaintances far from me,
You have made me an abomination, to them,
I am shut up, my eye wastes and I cannot see.

Lord I have called daily to You,
I have stretched out my hands to You,
Will You work wonders and raise the dead,
When they are dead, praising You they cannot do.

For Your loving kindness cannot in the grave be praised,
Nor Your faithfulness too,
How can Your wonders be known in the dark?

Can Your righteousness in the dark be on view?

But to You I have cried out O Lord,
And in the morning my prayer is to You,
Lord why do You cast off my soul?
Why do You hide Your face from my view?"

PSALM 89

"*I will sing of the mercies of the Lord,*
My mouth will make Your faithfulness known,
For I have said, 'Mercy shall be built up forever,'
Your faithfulness in the heavens be shown.

I have made a covenant with My chosen,
I have sworn by My servant David, I own,
Your seed I will establish forever,
For all generations build up your throne.

And the heavens will praise Your wonders O Lord,
Your faithfulness in the saints assembly,
Who among the mighty can be likened to the Lord?
Who in the heavens compared to the Lord can be?

God is greatly to be feared among the saints,
To be held in reverence by all around Him,
For You are the mighty one O God,
And the Most High cannot tolerate sin.

O Lord God who is mighty like You?
Your faithfulness O Lord surrounds You,
You rule the raging waves of the sea,
Stilling the waves is what You do.

The heavens are Yours, the earth also Yours,
The world in its fullness founded by You,
The north and the south You created them,

Using Your mighty arm in all You do.

Righteousness and justice are the foundation of Your throne,
Mercy and truth go before Your face,
Blessed are the people who know the joyful sound,
They walk in the continual light of Your grace.

In Your name they rejoice all day long,
In Your righteousness they praise away,
For You are the glory of their strength,
Our shield belongs to the Lord every day.

Our kings belong to the Holy One of Israel,
Then You spoke in a vision to Your holy one,
And said, "I have given help to one who is mighty,
And David I have exalted as My chosen son.

The enemy shall not outwit him,
Nor the son of wickedness him afflict,
I will beat down his foes before his face,
To those who hate and plague I will be strict.

My faithfulness and mercy will be with him,
His strength exalted in My name,
Also I will set his hand over the seas,
His right hand over rivers the same.

He shall cry to me, 'You are my Father,
My Rock and salvation's birth.'
Then I will make him my firstborn,
The highest of the kings of the earth.

My mercy shall keep him forever,
With My covenant he shall not be alone,
His seed I will make endue forever,
As the days of heaven will be his throne.

If his sons forsake My laws,
If they do not walk in judgements of mine,

If they break My statutes and commandments,
My punishment for them will not be fine.

For I will not break My faithful covenant,
Nor My loving kindness will I take,
Nor alter the word that has gone from My mouth,
His seed shall endure forever and his throne for My sake."

BOOK 4

Psalms 90-106 v 48

PSALM 90

"Lord You have been our refuge in generations,
Before even mountains were brought forth,
Or even before You had formed the world or the earth,
From everlasting to everlasting O God is Your worth.

You turn man to destruction saying to him, "Return!"
O children of men a thousand years in your sight,
Are like yesterday when it is past,
You carry them away like a flood in the watch of the night.

For we have been consumed by Your anger,
And by Your wrath we are terrified,
You have set our iniquities before You,
Our sins are no secret in You light.

For all our days pass away in Your wrath,
We finish our years with a sigh,
The days of our lives are seventy years,
And if we have strength eighty pass by.

Yet the boast is only labour and sorrow,
For it is soon cut off and we fly away,
Who knows the power of Your anger,
So teach us how to number each day.

That we may gain a heart of wisdom,
So that we may be glad and rejoice in our days,
Return O Lord and have compassion on Your people,

Make us glad to walk in Your ways.

Let Your work appear to Your servants,
And Your glory to the children of the land,
And let the beauty of the Lord be upon us,
Yes establish again the works of Your hand."

PSALM 91

"He who dwells in the secret place of the Most High,
And abides under the All Mighty shadow,
I will say of the Lord, 'He is my refuge and fortress,
My God and in Him my trust will go.'

He will deliver me from the fowlers snare,
And from the perilous pestilence,
He will cover me with His feathers,
His shield and buckler will be my defense.

I will not be afraid of the terror of night,
Nor the arrow that flies by day,
Nor of the pestilence that walks in darkness,
Nor of the destruction that wastes away.

A thousand may fall at my side,
And ten thousand at my right hand fall too,
But it shall not come anywhere near me,
The reward of the wicked my eyes will view.

Because I have set the Lord as my refuge,
The Most High is my dwelling place,
No evil thing shall befall me,
Of plagues there will be no trace.

For the Lord has put His angels in charge,
To keep me in all of my ways,
They with their hands will bear me up,

Keeping the stones from my feet away.

"Because you have set your love on Me,
I will deliver you and set you on high,
I will always answer your cry to Me,
My salvation and honour to you apply."

I want you to know dear reader,
The last verse is what the Lord says,
All of His promises are for you,
When you accept Jesus and give Him your praise.

God bless,

Trish Bishop

PSALM 92

"It is good to give thanks to the Lord,
To sing praises O Most High to Your name,
To declare Your loving kindness in the morning,
And Your faithfulness every night the same.

We sing praises to Your name O Lord,
On an instrument of ten strings play,
On a lute and a harp make harmonious sound,
For Your works make us glad every day.

O Lord how great are Your works,
Your thoughts are the very deepest,
A senseless man does not know,
Nor a fool understand the rest.

But You O Lord are on high forever,
O Lord behold Your enemy,
For all Your enemies shall perish,
Scattered the workers of iniquity will be.

But my strength You have exalted,
With fresh oil anointed I have been,
My ear hears my desire on the wicked,
My eyes the desire on my enemy has seen.

The righteous shall flourish as a palm tree,
They shall grow like a cedar in Lebanon,
Those who are planted in the Lord's house,

Shall in the courts of God belong.

They shall bear fruit in old age,
They shall be fresh and flourishing,
To declare that the Lord is upright,
He is my rock and there is no unrighteousness in Him."

PSALM 93

"The Lord reigns, He has girded Himself with strength,
The Lord is also clothed with majesty,
Your throne is established from old,
From everlasting You will always be.

The floods have lifted up O Lord,
The Lord is mightier than these,
They lift the voices of the waves,
Higher than the mighty waves of the seas.

You are the Mighty One O Lord,
Your testimonies are sure forever,
Holiness adorns Your house,
From this we will not sever."

PSALM 94

"O Lord to whom vengeance belongs,
O judge of the earth render punishment to the proud,
O God to whom judgement belongs shine forth,
Lord how long will the wicked triumph aloud?

They utter speech and speak insolent things,
They murder the fatherless, the widow and the stranger,
They say, "The Lord does not see nor does God understand,
Else the God of Jacob would show His anger."

Understand you senseless among the people,
And you fools when will you be wise?
He who made the ear, shall He not hear?
He also sees because He formed the eyes.

The Lord who has made all things,
Shall all nations instruct and correct,
The Lord teaches man knowledge,
The thoughts of man are futile and have no effect.

Blessed is the man taught Your law O Lord,
For You give him rest from days of adversity,
Until a pit is dug for the wicked,
And man's freedom from the wicked will be.

The Lord will not cast off His people,
Nor his inheritance will He forsake,
But judgment will return to the righteous,

The upright His law will not break.

Who will rise up for me against evildoers?
Who will stand against workers of iniquity?
Unless the Lord had been my help,
My soul soon settled in silence would be.

Shall the throne of iniquity devise evil,
And have fellowship Lord with You?
They gather against the life of the righteous,
The condemnation of innocent blood they do.

But The Lord is my rock and defense,
My rock and the God of my defense,
He has brought on them their iniquity,
He cut them off for their wickedness was huge."

PSALM 95

"O come let us sing to the Lord,
For the rock of salvation joyfully shout,
Yes let us joyfully shout to Him in psalms,
His greatness is what this is all about.

For the Lord God is a great God,
Above all gods He is the great King,
In His hand are the deep places of the earth,
Let us worship and praise as we sing.

Let us kneel before the Lord our maker,
We are the sheep of His pasture too,
We are the work of His holy hand,
O God Most High, may we be worthy of You?"

"Do not harden your heart in the rebellion,
Do not go either astray in your heart,
As in the day of trial in the wilderness,
Your fathers tested me from the start.

For forty years I was grieved with that generation,
They did not know My way was the best,
So I swore My wrath and anger,
They shall never enter into My rest."

PSALM 96

"O come let us sing to the Lord,
Sing to the Lord of all the earth,
Sing to the Lord and bless His name,
Proclaim the good news of salvation,
With all of your worth.

Declare His glory among the nations,
For the Lord is great and greatly to be praised,
All the gods of the people are only idols,
The Lord in all His glory is to be raised

Give to the Lord O families of people,
Give to the Lord the glory of His name,
O worship the Lord in the beauty of holiness,
Let Your praise and worship be always the same.

Say among the nations, 'The Lord reigns,
Let the heavens rejoice and the earth be glad,
Let the sea roar in all its fullness,
Let the fields be joyful in all that can be had!'

Then all the trees rejoice in the woods,
For the Lord is coming to judge the earth,
He will judge the world with righteousness,
And the people with His truth and full worth."

PSALM 97

"The Lord reigns, let the earth rejoice,
Let the multitude of isles be so glad,
Clouds of darkness surround Him now,
And a fire burns up His enemies so bad.

His lightening's light up the world,
The earth sees mountains like wax melt,
The heavens declare His righteousness,
The presence of the Lord on the earth is felt.

Let all be put to shame who serve carved images,
Who boast in idols, gods they are called too,
Worship the Lord you gods and make Zion glad,
All the people will see His glory in the heavens view.

The daughters of Judah then rejoice,
For You O Lord are the Most High,
Above all the earth You are exalted,
That You are above all gods we cannot deny.

You who love the Lord , hate evil,
For He preserves all His saints too,
He delivers them out of the hands of the wicked,
And gladness for the upright He gives to you."

PSALM 98

"O sing to the Lord a new song,
For He has done marvelous things,
His holy arm and right hand give Him victory,
The whole earth joyfully sings.

He has remembered His faithfulness to Israel,
His righteousness is revealed in nations too,
All the ends of the earth shall see salvation,
Joyfully shout praise is what we must do.

Break forth into song, rejoice singing praise,
With the strings of a harp to the Lord sing,
With the sound of a psalm and the harp,
Shout joyful praise to the great King.

Let the sea roar in all its fullness,
The world and all who dwell in it,
Let the rivers clap their hands,
May the whole world in God's light be lit.

Let all the hills be joyful together,
For the Lord's judgement of earth will soon be,
With all of God's judgement and righteousness,
He will judge all the people with equity."

PSALM 99

"The Lord reigns let the people tremble,
He dwells between the Cherubim,
The Lord is so great in Zion,
High above all things people see Him.

Let them praise Your awesome name,
For holy and full of strength is the King,
You are exalted O Lord our God,
Justice and righteousness to Jacob You bring.

Moses and Aaron were among Your priests,
Samuel also was among those called by Your name,
They called upon the Lord, You answered them,
Your ordinance and testimony they kept just the same.

You answered them O Lord our God,
You were to them the GOD WHO FORGIVES,
Exalt the Lord our God, worship Him,
Each one worship the Lord as long as he lives."

PSALM 100

"Make a joyful shout to the Lord,
Serve the Lord with gladness all you lands,
Come before His presence with singing,
Singing praise with the clapping of hands.

Know that the Lord, He is God,
We in the pastures are His sheep,
It is He who made us not we ourselves,
Therefore His statutes we will keep.

Enter into His gates with thanksgiving,
And into His courts with praise,
Be thankful to Him and praise His name,
For the Lord is good and in mercy,
Our souls He does raise."

PSALM 101

"I will sing of mercy and justice to You O Lord,
I will sing praises and behave wisely in a perfect way,
I will walk within my house with a perfect heart,
When will You come to me? I will wait and not go astray.

I will set nothing wicked before my eyes,
Wickedness shall not ever cling to me,
A perverse heart shall depart from me,
And knowledge of wickedness shall not be.

Whoever secretly slanders his neighbour,
Him I will destroy as one not pure,
The one who has a haughty and proud heart,
Him I will never at all endure.

My eyes shall be on the faithful of the land,
That they may dwell well with Me,
He who works deceit shall not be in my house,
But he who walks in a perfect way shall be."

PSALM 102

"Hear my prayer O Lord as unto You I cry,
Hide not Your face in my troubled day,
Incline Your ear to me O Lord I plead,
On the day I call in Your mercy answer right away.

For my days are consumed like smoke,
My heart is stricken like withered grass,
My bones are burnt like a hearth,
O let not the sound of my groaning pass.

I am like a pelican in the wilderness,
And like an owl in the desert lie awake,
And like a sparrow on the housetop,
All my sorrows O Lord please take.

My enemies reproach me all day long,
Those who deride swear on oath against me,
For I have eaten ashes like bread,
My drink mingled with tears will be.

Because of Your indignation and wrath,
You lift me up and cast me away,
And I wither away like the grass,
Like a shadow that lengthens is my day.

But You O Lord shall endure forever,
Generations will remember Your name,
You will arise and have mercy on Zion,

Your love for Zion is always the same.

For the Lord shall build up Zion,
Of the cry of the destitute He will be aware,
All the peoples will gather together,
The name of God in Zion they will declare."

PSALM 103

"Bless the Lord O my soul,
And all that is in me bless His holy name,
Forget not all the Lord's benefits,
And bless the Lord my soul again.

Who forgives all your iniquities,
Who heals all your diseases too,
Who redeems your life from destruction,
Gives the crown of loving kindness to you.

So bless the Lord for His benefits,
For He satisfies your mouth with good things,
So your mouth is restored like an eagles,
For He is Lord and King of all Kings.

The Lord executes righteousness,
And justice for all the oppressed,
He made known His ways to Moses,
So that the children of Israel were blessed.

The Lord is merciful and gracious,
Slow to anger and abounding in mercy is He,
He will not always strive with us,
Nor punish according to iniquity.

For as the heavens are high above the earth,
So is His mercy to those whose fear of Him is great,
As far as the east is from the west,

He will remove our transgressions if we wait.

As for man his days are like grass,
Like a flower he flourishes in a field,
But the wind blows and it is gone,
To forgetfulness it will yield.

But the mercy of the Lord is everlasting,
And His righteousness to children's children,
To such as keep the covenant,
And remembers His commands to keep them.

Bless the Lord all His angels,
Heeding the voice of His word,
Bless the Lord you all His hosts,
And you ministers, bless with one accord."

PSALM 104

"O Lord my God You are very great,
You are clothed in honour and majesty,
You cover Yourself with a garment of light,
Stretched in the heavens like curtains they will be.

He makes the clouds His chariots,
Who walks on the winds wings,
Who makes His angels spirits,
His ministers like flames of fire springs.

You who laid the foundation of earth,
So moved forever it would not be,
You covered it with the deep, like a garment,
And that is how You made the sea.

The waters stood above the mountains,
At the voice of Your thunder hastened away,
They went up over the mountains,
Then went down to the valley to stay.

The Lord waters the hills from upper places,
All His works satisfy the whole earth,
He causes grass to grow for the cattle,
The Lord supplies with all His worth.

And vegetation He causes to grow for man,
That he may bring from the earth his food,
And the wine that makes man's heart glad,

Oil to make his face shine so good.

The cedars of Lebanon which He planted,
Where the birds do make their nests,
The stork has her home in the fir trees,
The cliffs are where the rock badger rests.

He appoints the moon for the seasons,
The sun knows when to go down,
You make the darkness then it is night,
When all the beasts in the forest creep around.

The young lions roar after their prey,
And from God their food they seek,
When the sun rises they gather together,
And lie down in their dens to sleep.

I will sing to the Lord as long as I live,
I will sing praises to God while I have my being,
May my meditation of Him be sweet,
For it is God's help and love I am seeing."

PSALM 105

"O give thanks to the Lord,
And call upon His name,
To the people make known His deeds,
Sing psalms and praise to Him proclaim,

Talk of His wondrous works,
And glory in His holy name,
Let all hearts rejoice and seek the Lord,
For all of His works once again.

Remember always His marvelous works,
O seed of Abraham and Jacob's too,
He remembers His covenant forever,
And all His promises to you.

When they went from nation to nation,
From one kingdom to another too,
God permitted not one to do them wrong,
Saying, "Touch My anointed you must not do!"

Moreover He called for a famine in the land,
He destroyed all provision of bread,
He sent Joseph who was sold as a slave,
Through him all his family was fed.

They had hurt Joseph's feet with fetters,
In prison he was in irons laid,
The word of the Lord tested him,

He trusted God and was never afraid.

The king of Egypt sent and released him,
The ruler of the people set him free,
And made him lord over his house,
Ruler of all his possessions he would be.

Israel and family also came to Egypt,
And Jacob dwelt in the land of Ham,
He increased his people greatly,
So to be rid of them Egypt had a plan.

God sent Moses His servant,
And Aaron his brother too,
He gave them signs for the Egyptians,
And told them both what to do.

They brought out His people with joy,
His chosen ones with gladness grew,
He gave them the Gentiles land to live in,
With all His laws and statutes too."

PSALM 106

"O give thanks to the Lord for He is good,
Forever His mercy endures for you,
Who can utter the mighty acts of the Lord,
He who at all times righteous things does do?

O Lord all favour You have toward Your people,
O visit me with Your salvation at last,
That I may see the benefit of Your chosen ones,
And may glory in Your inheritance.

We have sinned with our fathers,
Done wickedly and committed iniquity,
In Egypt our Fathers did not understand Your ways,
And rebelled at the Red Sea.

Nevertheless He saved them,
All for His names sake set free,
That He might make His power known,
He rebuked them, then dried up the Red Sea.

He led them through the depths,
And through the wilderness too,
He saved them from the hand of the enemy,
Once they over the Red Sea went through.

The waters covered their enemies,
There was not one of them left,
Then they believed and praised the lord,

The Egyptians were all bereft.

But they soon forgot God's works,
For His counsel they did not wait,
But lusted exceedingly in the wilderness,
God tested them in the desert,
But they learned their lesson too late.

They made a golden calf in Horeb,
And worshipped the image there,
Their glory became the image of an ox that eats grass,
They forgot their Saviour but did not care.

God had done great things in Egypt,
Wondrous works in the land of Ham,
Awesome things by the Red Sea,
God was very angry but Moses soothed the I Am,

Then they despised the pleasant land,
They did not believe God's word,
Murmured and complained in their tents,
And did not heed the voice of the Lord.

Because they did not listen,
To all God in His mercy had said,
They did not see the promised land,
And wondered forty years in the wilderness instead."

BOOK 5

Psalms 107-150 v 6

PSALM 107

"O give thanks to the Lord for He is good,
And His mercies forever endure,
Let the redeemed of the Lord say so,
For their redemption is very sure.

Whom He has redeemed from the enemy,
And redeemed from all the enemies hand,
From the east and west, north and south,
He has gathered them from all of the land.

They wandered in the wilderness,
They found no city to dwell in on the way,
Hungry and thirsty they were so faint,
They cried to the Lord to take their trouble away.

He delivered them out of their distresses,
On the right way forth He led them,
That they might go to a dwelling place,
O give thanks to the Lord for His mercy to men.

Those who sat in darkness in the shadow of death,
Who despised the counsel of the Most High,
They rebelled against the words of God,
Although He had put away their trouble,
When they unto Him did cry.

He brought them out of the shadow of death,
And broke their chains all in pieces,

O that man would give thanks to the Lord,
And praise Him for their releases.

Fools because of their transgressions and iniquity,
Were afflicted and could not eat any food,
They cried out to the Lord in their distress,
And He saved them again which was so good.

He sent His word out and it healed them,
From destruction He delivered them,
O that men would give thanks for His goodness,
For His wonderful works to the children of men.

O that men would give thanks and praise,
Let them sacrifice the sacrifice of thanksgiving,
And come before Him with rejoicing,
And declare the Lord's works to the living.

He can turn rivers into a wilderness,
And water springs into dry ground,
A fruitful land into barrenness,
Wherever the wicked ones are found.

He then turns dry land into water springs,
There He makes the hungry to dwell,
That they may establish a dwelling place,
And yield a fruitful harvest as well.

He sets the poor on high from affliction,
Like flocks together makes their families,
All iniquity now stops its mouth,
They once more all live in peace."

PSALM 108

"O God my heart is steadfast in praise,
With lute and harp I will awake,
I will praise You O Lord among the people,
I will magnify Your truth and Your statutes not break.

God has spoken in His holiness,
I will rejoice and Shecham divide,
Gilead and Manneseph are mine,
All of my assets I will not hide.

For Ephraim is the helmet for my head,
Over Edom I will cast my shoe,
Judah is my lawgiver and Moab my wash pot,
And over Philistia I will triumph too.

Who will bring me into the strong city?
For You O God have not gone with our armies,
Man's help is useless, Give us Your help O Lord,
For You alone will tread down our enemies."

PSALM 109

"Do not keep silence O God of my praise,
For deceitful mouths open against me,
They speak against me with lying tongues,
Surrounding me with hatred they will be.

In return for my love they are my accusers,
But prayer is the answer I will give,
Thus they reward evil for good,
Go against my love as long as they live.

Set a wicked man over him,
And an accuser at his right hand,
When he is judged let him be found guilty,
Let another take his office and reason to stand.

Let the iniquity of his father be remembered,
And let not his mother's sin be blotted out,
Let them be continually before the Lord,
And let the Lord not hear their shout.

Because he did not remember to show mercy,
But persecuted the poor and needy men,
That he may slay the broken in heart,
Let his cursing return to him then.

For he clothed himself with cursing like a garment,
So let it like water enter him,
Let it be like the garment that covers,

Like oil in his bones is his evil sin.

You O Lord deal with me for your name's sake,
O God because Your mercy is good, deliver me,
For I am poor and needy O Lord,
My poor heart wounded within me will be.

Help me O Lord my God,
Save me according to Your mercy,
That they may know this is Your hand,
That You Lord have done it for me.

Yes I will greatly praise the Lord,
For He stands at the right hand of the poor,
I will praise Him among the multitude,
My praise and worship will be evermore."

PSALM 110

"The Lord said to my Lord,
Come sit at My right hand,
'Til I make Your enemies Your footstool,
In the midst of Your enemies Your rule will stand.

In the beauty of holiness in the morning,
You have the dew of Your youth like a shower,
Your people shall be volunteers,
In the day of Your great power.

The Lord has sworn and will not relent,
Your priesthood is forever like Melchizedek,
The Lord is always at Your right hand,
And will keep all Your enemies in check."

PSALM 111

"I will praise the Lord with my whole heart,
And praise Him in the congregations,
He has declared to His people His power,
By giving them the heritage of the nations.

The works of the Lord are great,
Studied by all who have pleasure in them,
His work is honourable and glorious,
All from His righteousness and love will stem.

All His people are truly sure,
That forever they will stand,
They are one in righteousness and truth,
His covenant forever under His command.

The fear of the Lord is the beginning,
Of wisdom and good understandings,
For all of those who obey Him,
His praise is forever for He is the King of Kings."

PSALM 112

"Bless the man who fears the Lord,
Who delights greatly in His command,
His descendants will be mighty on earth,
And be blessed as long as they stand.

Wealth and riches will be in his house,
And his righteousness endures forever,
The upright see the light in the darkness,
He will not be shaken no, never.

He is gracious and full of compassion,
A good man deals with grace and lends,
He will guide his affairs with discretion,
His trust in the lord never ends.

The righteous are remembered everlastingly,
In the Lord his heart will always trust,
So that he will never be afraid,
To see his desires on his enemy he must.

He has always given to the poor,
His righteousness endures forevermore,
His strength be exalted forever,
But the wicked perish under the law."

PSALM 113

"Praise O servants of the Lord,
Praise His Holy name,
Blessed be the Lord's name forever,
From the rising of the sun,
And the going down of the same.

The Lord is high above the heavens,
His glory above the heavens too,
Who is like the Lord our God,
Who shows mercy and grace to you?

He who dwells up on high,
Humbles Himself to behold,
The things of the earth all around,
All are in His hand to hold.

He raises the poor out of the dust,
And lifts the needy out of the ash heap,
That He may seat him with princes,
Grant a mother and children a place to sleep."

PSALM 114

"When Israel went out of Egypt,
And Jacob from people of a strange tongue,
Judah became His sure sanctuary,
Israel's dominion he had won.

The sea saw it and fled, Jordan was driven back,
The mountains skipped like rams,
Why did Jordan turn back and the sea flee,
While the little hills skipped like the lambs?

Tremble O earth at the Lord's presence,
At the presence of the God of Jacob too,
Who once turned rock into water,
Turned flint into a fountain He did do."

PSALM 115

"Not unto us O Lord not unto us,
Let all glory be unto Your name,
Because of Your mercy and truth give glory,
Our praise and worship be ever the same.

The Gentiles say, 'Where is their God?'
Because we cannot hold You in our hand,
Their gods are made of silver and gold,
But You O God abide in heaven not on the land.

Their gods are the work of their hands,
They have mouths but do not speak,
They have eyes and do not see,
They have ears with no hearing,
And a nose with no smelling,
Their power does not exist, is not just weak.

The have hands but do not handle,
Feet they have but do not walk,
Those who make them are like them,
They are as dead in spite of all their talk.

O Israel trust only in the lord,
For He is your help and shield,
O house of Aaron trust the Lord,
For God's help for you is sealed.

May the Lord give you increase,

You and your children too,
May you be truly blessed by the Lord,
Who made heaven and earth for you.

The heavens all belong to the Lord,
The earth He has given to men,
The dead do not praise the Lord,
But we will praise and worship Him,
And our God will defend us then."

PSALM 116

"I love the Lord for He has heard,
Because He inclined His ear to me ,
Therefore I will call upon Him,
For Him my praise will always be.

The pains of death surround me,
Sheol almost had me in its hold,
I called upon the name of the Lord,
'O Lord I implore You save my soul.'

Gracious is the Lord and righteous,
I was brought low but He saved me,
The Lord preserves the simple at heart,
With us all He deals bountifully,

What shall I render to the Lord,
For all His benefits to me?
I will take up the cup of salvation,
And pay all my vows faithfully.

Precious in the sight of the Lord,
Is the death of His saints always,
O Lord I truly am Your servant,
And will serve You all of my days."

PSALM 117

"Praise the Lord all you Gentiles,
For His great mercy to you,
And for all of His kindness,
And for His truth give thanks too."

PSALM 118

"O give thanks to the Lord for He is good,
His mercies endure forever,
Let the house of Aaron say,
"His mercy endures forever!"
Let those who fear the Lord say,
"His mercy endures forever!"
And is for You every day.

I called on the Lord in my distress,
He answered and put me in a broad place,
The Lord is on my side whom shall I fear?
For I will not fall into disgrace.

It is better to trust in the Lord,
Than to put confidence in men,
All the nations surround me,
In the name of the Lord I will destroy them.

Yes they surround me like bees,
They were quenched as in a fire,
The Lord is my strength and song,
He is my salvation and my desire.

The right hand of the Lord is valiant,
I shall live and not die,
The Lord has chastened me severely,
But that He delivered me I can't deny.

The stone that the builders rejected,
Has become the chief cornerstone for you,
This, the Lord's doing is marvelous in our eyes,
For this is the day the Lord has made too.

You are my God and I will exalt You,
I will never stop praising You, no never,
O give thanks to the lord for He is good,
And His mercy endures forever."

PSALM 119

Aleph

"Blessed are the undefiled in the way,
Who walk in the law of the Lord.
Blessed are those keeping His testimony,
Who seek Him with one accord,
They also do no iniquity,
But walk in all of His way.
You have commanded us to keep Your precepts,
And keep Your statutes every day,
I will praise You with an upright heart,
I will keep Your statutes too,
As I learn Your righteous judgements,
I will always follow You.

Beth

How can a young man cleanse his way,
By heeding to all of Your word?
With my whole heart I have sought You,
Let me not wander from all I have heard.
Blessed are You O Lord, teach me Your statutes,
All of Your judgements are on my lips,
I will meditate on Your precepts,
All of Your testimonies on my heart sits.

Gimel

Deal bountifully with Your servant,
That I may live and keep Your word,
Open my eyes that I may see,
The wonders of Your law O Lord.
You rebuke the proud and cursed,
Who from Your commands stray,
Remove from me reproach and contempt,
For I keep Your testimonies each day.

Daleth

My soul O Lord clings to the dust,
Revive me according to Your word.
I have declared my ways, You answered.
Teach me Your statutes again O Lord.
Make me understand Your precepts,
On Your wonderful works I meditate,
My soul melts with heaviness,
To receive strength from You I wait.

He

Teach me O Lord the way of Your statutes,
And I shall keep them to the end.
Give me Your understanding to keep Your law,
Day and night in Your commands I spend.
Establish Your word to Your servant,
Who is devoted to hearing from You,
Turn away my reproach which I dread,
Longing for Your precepts I surely do.

Waw

Let Your mercies come also to me,
Your salvation according to Your word,
I will then have an answer to them who reproach,
For my trust is in You O Lord.
Take not the word of truth from my mouth,
Then I will keep Your law continually,
Forever and ever I will walk in liberty,
Speaking Your testimony before kings I will be.

Zayin

Remember the word to Your servant,
This is my comfort in affliction,
For Your word gives me life,
The proud have me in great division.
Your word shields me from their strife,
I remember Your name in the night.
O Lord I always keep Your laws,
They have become always mine.
Your precepts O Lord I adore.

Heth

You are my life my portion O Lord,
I have said I will keep Your word,
I entreat Your favour with my whole heart.
To turn away from You I cannot afford,
At midnight I arise to give You thanks,
I am companion to all who fear You,
And of those who keep Your precepts,

For the earth is full of Your mercy too.

Teth

You have dwelt well with Your servant,
O Lord according to Your word,
Teach me good judgement and knowledge,
The proud are against me with one accord.
Teach me Your statutes for You are good,
And I will keep Your precepts with my whole heart.
It is good for me to have been afflicted,
Because I came to You and made a good start.

Yod

Your hands have made and fashioned me,
Help me to learn all Your commands.
Those who fear You will be glad to see me,
For You have answered in Your mercy, all my demands.
I know O Lord Your judgements are right,
That in faithfulness You afflicted me,
Let Your merciful kindness be a comfort,
My delight always in Your word will be.

Kaph

My soul faints for Your salvation,
Saying 'When will You comfort me?'
I have been like a wineskin in smoke.
How many will the days of Your servant be?
When will You judge those who persecute me?
For the proud have dug pits for me,
Which I know goes against Your law,

When O Lord will Your deliverance be?

Lamed

Forever O Lord Your word is settled in heaven,
Your faithfulness endures forevermore,
You establish the earth and it abides,
It continues according to Your law.
Unless Your law had been my delight,
I would have perished because of strife,
I will never ever forget Your precepts,
For by them You have given me life.

Mem

O Lord how I love Your law,
It is my meditation every day,
They make me wiser than my enemy,
Who is ever there but now keeps away.
I have more understanding than my teachers,
Because I keep Your precepts every day,
I have not departed from Your judgements,
I have restrained my feet from going astray.

Nun

Your word is a lamp to my feet,
And to my path a bright light,
I have sworn and kept Your judgements,
Revive me O Lord with Your great might.
The wicked have laid a snare for me,
Yet from Your precepts I have not strayed,
For they are the rejoicing of my heart,

And in my heart they are forever laid.

Samek

I love Your law but hate the double minded,
You are my hiding place and my shield.
Depart from me you evildoers,
To the commandments of my God I yield.
Uphold me according to Your word,
Do not let my hope ashamed be,
Hold me up O Lord and I shall be safe,
I will uphold Your statutes eternally.

Ayin

I have done justice and righteousness,
To my oppressors, do not leave me,
For Your servant be surety for good,
Do not let me by the proud oppressed be.
My eyes fail from seeking Your salvation,
And Your righteous word too,
Deal with Your servant with mercy,
Teach me all Your statutes in all I do.

Pe

Your testimonies are wonderful O Lord,
Therefore my soul does well to keep them.
The entrance of Your word gives light,
Understanding even to simple men,
Direct my steps by Your word O Lord,
Let no iniquity have dominion over me.
Redeem me from the oppression of man,
You O Lord my deliverer be.

Tsadde

Righteous are You O Lord,
Your judgements are upright too,
Your testimonies which You have commanded,
Are as righteous and faithful as You.
Trouble and anguish overtake me,
Yet Your commandments are my delight,
The righteousness of Your testimonies are everlasting,
With understanding I live in Your light.

Goph

I cry out with my whole heart,
'Hear me O Lord I keep Your statutes in every way.'
I cry out to You, 'Save me!'
Your testimony I keep and I arise before the dawning of the day.
My eyes are awake through the night watches,
That I may meditate on Your word,
Hear me to Your loving kindness,
Revive me again O Lord.

Resh

Consider my affliction and deliver me,
Plead my cause and redeem me,
Revive me according to Your word,
My salvation from the wicked will be.
Many are my persecutors and enemies,
Yet from Your testimonies I do not turn,
I see the treacheries and I am disquieted,
But the truth of Your word I soon learn.

Shin

Princes persecute me without a cause,
But my heart is still in awe of Your word,
I rejoice as one who has found great treasure.
Iniquity and lying I abhor O Lord.
Great peace have those who love Your law,
For nothing causes them to stumble It's true.
Lord I hope always for Your salvation,
And my soul keeps Your commandments too.

Tav

Let my cry come before You O Lord,
Give me understanding of Your true word,
Let my supplication come before You,
My tongue speaks greatly of You O Lord.
My lips shall utter praise for Your statutes,
For I have chosen Your precepts too,
I long for Your salvation O Lord,
Let my soul live and it will praise You."

PSALM 120

"In my distress I called to the Lord,
Who heard me and delivered me,
He delivered me from lying lips,
My Saviour He will always be.

What shall be given to the false tongue,
Whatever shall be done to you?
Sharp arrows off the warriors bow,
Or will fire from the broom tree do?

Woe is for me for I dwell in Meshech,
And dwell amongst the tents of Kedar,
I dwelt with those too long who hate peace,
Against peace they war and go too far."

PSALM 121

"I will lift my eyes to the hills,
For my help comes from there,
My help comes truly from the Lord,
Who made the heavens and earth for our care.

He will not allow your foot to be moved,
He will not slumber while you He keeps,
Behold He will always keep Israel,
For He neither slumbers nor sleeps.

The Lord is your keeper forever,
He is a shade at your right hand,
The sun will not strike you by day,
Nor the moon at night where you stand.

The Lord will preserve you from evil,
He will keep your soul from sin,
From this time forth and forevermore,
The Lord will preserve your going out,
And your coming in."

PSALM 122

"I was so glad when they said to me,
"Let us go into the house of the Lord!"
Our feet are standing within Your gates,
O Jerusalem give heed to the Lord's word.

As a city compacted together is Jerusalem,
Where the Lord's tribes praise His name,
For thrones are set there for judgement,
They are the thrones of David, the same.

All pray for the peace of Jerusalem,
May they prosper all who love you,
Peace and prosperity be within your walls,
Seeking good is what we shall do."

PSALM 123

"Unto You in the heavens I lift my eyes,
As the eyes of a servant look to a masters hand,
As the eyes of a maiden to her mistress,
Our eyes look to the Lord God of our land.

Have mercy on us O Lord have mercy,
We are filled with the contempt that exceeds,
Our soul is filled with the scorn of those at ease,
And the contempt of the proud we do heed."

PSALM 124

"If the Lord had not been on our side,
Come now let Israel say this too,
Because the Lord was on our side,
We were not swallowed up,
Fight for us the Lord did do.

When men rose up against us,
Waters would have covered our soul,
Swollen waters would have swallowed up us,
Then we would have been no longer whole.

Blessed be the Lord who has not made us prey,
We escaped like a bird from the snare,
The snare is broken and we escaped,
That the Lord is our help, we are well aware."

PSALM 125

"Those who trust the Lord,
Are the same as Zion's mount,
Which cannot be moved, it abides forever,
As the surrounding mountains,
Which he cannot count.

For the scepter of wickedness shall not rest,
On the land of the righteous it shall not be,
For that land to them only is allotted,
Lest they fall again into iniquity.

Do good O Lord to those who do good,
To those with an upright heart,
For such turn away from wicked ways,
With workers of iniquity take no part."

PSALM 126

"When the Lord brought back Zion,
Out of captivity brought He them,
We were like those who are in a dream,
Our mouths filled with laughter then.

Our hearts were singing too,
Among the nations they did say,
"The Lord has done great things for them!"
And we are full of gladness today.

Those who sow in many tears,
Shall be joyful as they reap,
He who weeps bears seed for sowing,
And shall rejoice in the blessing he does keep."

PSALM 127

"Unless the Lord the house does build,
They labour in vain who build it,
Unless the Lord guards their city,
The watchman watches for no benefit.

It vain for you to early rise,
And to sit up very late too,
For you will eat the bread of sorrow,
But as God's beloved He gives sleep to you.

Behold children are a gift from the Lord,
The fruit of the womb rewards will be,
Like the arrows in the hands of a warrior,
So the children of your youth happily.

Happy is the man whose quiver is full,
He will never be ashamed of them,
But speak with their enemy at the gate,
For they will be protected then."

PSALM 128

"Blessed is everyone who fears the Lord,
Who walks in all of His ways,
When you eat the labour of your hands,
You shall be happy and well, all your days.

Your wife shall be like a fruitful vine,
Children like olive plants around your table sit,
Your wife the very heart of your house,
Because you fear the Lord, you are blessed in it.

And may you see the good of Jerusalem,
All the days of your life,
That you may see your children's children,
Israel will have peace and no more strife."

PSALM 129

"Let Israel say, "They have afflicted me from my youth,"
Yet have not prevailed against me,
The plougher ploughed on my back,
The furrows as long as could be,
The Lord has cut the cords of the wicked,
For He does all things righteously.

Let all those who hate Zion,
Be put to shame and turned back,
Let them be as grass on the housetops,
That wither for the nourishment they lack.

Which the reaper cannot fill his hands with,
Nor fill the arms of he who binds sheaves,
Neither let he who passes by say,
Bless you in the name of the Lord before he leaves."

PSALM 130

"Out of the depths I cry to You O Lord,
Lord please hear my voice,
Let Your ears hear my supplications,
Answer me so I may rejoice.

If You O Lord mark iniquities,
O Lord how can anyone stand,
But I know You are full of forgiveness,
And mercy for us always in Your hand.

I wait for the Lord as my soul waits,
More than those in the morning watch wait,
Yes more than those who watch in the morning,
My hope in the Lord is a watchful state.

O Israel hope now in the Lord,
For in the Lord mercy will always be,
In Him is abundant redemption,
He shall redeem Israel from iniquity."

PSALM 131

"Lord my heart is not haughty,
Nor my eyes lofty in me,
I do not concern with great matters,
Nor things that profound may be.

Surely I have calmed and quieted,
Like a child by his mother is weaned,
Like a weaned child is my soul within me,
O Israel on the Lord in hope I have leaned."

PSALM 132

"Lord remember David's afflictions,
How he swore and vowed to the Lord,
He vowed to the Mighty One of Jacob,
To continue always to obey His word.

Surely I will not go into my house,
Or into the comfort of my bed,
I will not give sleep to my eyes,
Until I find a place for the Lord instead.

Behold we heard it in Ephrathah,
And found it in the woods and fields,
Let us go into Your Tabernacle,
At Your footstool everyone kneels.

Arise O Lord to Your resting place,
You and the strength You employ,
Let Your priests be clothed in righteousness,
And Your saints shouting with joy.

The Lord has sworn in truth to David,
And He will not turn from it,
"I will set your sons upon your throne,
And on it they will always sit!"

The Lord has chosen Zion,
He has declared it for His dwelling place,
"I will dwell here for I have desired it,

And will bless all who seek My face.

I will abundantly bless her provision,
I will satisfy Zion's poor with bread,
I will clothe her priests with salvation,
And bring glory over their head.

I will make the strength of David grow,
And prepare for My anointed a lamp,
His enemies I will clothe with shame,
And David's throne will flourish in his camp."

PSALM 133

"Behold how good and pleasant it is,
For brothers to dwell in unity,
It is like precious oil on the beard of Aaron,
Running down his garments so freely.

It is like the dew of Hermon,
Descending from Zion to the shore,
For there the Lord commanded a blessing,
A blessing for ever more."

PSALM 134

Behold and bless the Lord,
All you servants of the Lord,
Who by night are in the house of the Lord,
Lift up your hands with one accord.

The Lord bless you in the sanctuary,
For His blessing you can rely on,
The Lord who made the heavens and earth,
Will bless you all from mount Zion."

PSALM 135

"Praise the Lord, praise the name of the Lord,
Praise Him O you servants of the Lord,
You who stand in the courts of our God,
Praise Him again and again for His word.

Sing praises to His name for it is pleasant,
The Lord has chosen Jacob for Himself too,
And Israel for His special treasure,
Praise Him for all He has done for you.

For I know that the Lord is great,
And our Lord is above all gods it is true,
Whatever He pleases He does on heaven and earth,
He causes vapours to fall out of view.

He destroyed the firstborn of Egypt,
Both man and every beast He did do,
He sent many signs and wonders to Egypt,
Upon Pharaoh and his servants too.

He slew mighty kings and defeated nations,
Sihon, king of the Amorites and Og, king of Bashan,
And all the kingdoms of Canaan,
And he gave their land to His people Israel,
To live there and do the best they can.

Your name O Lord endures forever,
Through all generations is Your fame,

For the Lord will judge His people justly,
Having compassion on all who love His name.

Bless the Lord O house of Israel,
Bless the Lord house of Aaron too,
Bless the Lord O house of Levi,
Those who fear the Lord will bless Him anew."

PSALM 136

"O give thanks to the Lord for He is good,
And His mercy endures forever,
O give thanks for He is God of all gods,
His mercy never ends no, never.

To Him who does great wonders,
To Him who laid out the earth,
His mercy endures forever,
To Him who gave the stars their birth.

His mercy endures forever,
To Him who made great lights,
His mercy endures forever,
He made the sun to rule by day,
And the moon to rule the night.

To Him who struck Egypt's firstborn,
His mercy endures forever,
He brought Israel out from among them,
His mercy endures forever.

His mercy endures forever,
With a strong hand and an outstretched arm,
His mercy endures forever,
And He saves His people from harm.

He who divided the Red sea in two,
His mercy endures forever,

Then on dry land He led Israel through,
His mercy endures forever.

His mercy endures forever,
For He remembers our lowly state,
He rescues us from our enemies,
And we did not have long to wait.

That His mercy endures forever,
On this we can surely bank,
As His mercy is always for us is sure,
We must always give praise and our thanks."

PSALM 137

"By the rivers of Babylon,
Where we sat down and wept,
We remembered Zion,
Where in peace we slept.

We all hung our harps up,
Upon the willow trees,
Our captives asked us for a song,
But they wanted only to tease.

How could we sing the Lord's song,
In the land of captivity?
We will not forget you O Jerusalem,
Not amongst all this iniquity.

Let my tongue cling to my mouth,
Lest I forget to exalt Jerusalem,
Remember against all the sons of Edom,
And for their wickedness repay them."

PSALM 138

"I will praise You with my whole heart,
Before the gods I will sing praise to You,
I will worship towards Your holy Temple O God,
For the loving kindness and mercy You do.

You magnified Your word above Your name,
In the days when I cried out,
You answered me and made me bold,
And gave me the strength to shout.

Though I walk in the midst of trouble,
You will always revive me,
Your right hand will save me,
As You stretch Your hand against my enemy.

The Lord will perfect that which concerns me,
For His mercy endures forever,
And He will forever be my strength and shield,
And His works will last forever."

PSALM 139

"O Lord You have searched me,
And have known me in all my ways,
You understand my every thought,
And watch over all my days.

O Lord God You know everything,
That I ever do or say,
You have hedged me before and behind me,
I cannot contain Your words every day.

Where can I go from Your Spirit,
From Your presence I cannot flee,
If I ascend to heaven You are there,
If I make my bed in hell, there You will be.

If I take the wings of the morning,
And dwell in the uttermost part of the sea,
Even there Your right hand will hold me,
And safe in Your hands I will be.

You formed me in my mother's womb,
I am fearfully and wonderfully made,
I will praise You O Lord for all Your works,
For in You I will never be afraid.

Your works, my soul knows very well,
My frame was not hidden from You,
Your eyes saw my substance yet unformed,

In Your book I am fully on view.

How precious are Your thoughts to me,
O God how great the sum of them too,
They are more in number than the sand,
When I awake I am still with You.

O that You would slay the wicked O God,
Depart from me you bloodthirsty men,
For you always take God's name in vain,
I hate those who hate You,
For on You O Lord I depend.

Search me O God and know my heart,
Try me and know my anxiety,
See if there is in me any wickedness,
Lead me to an everlasting way to be."

PSALM 140

"Deliver me O Lord from evil men,
Preserve me from violent men too,
Who plan evil things in their hearts,
For that is what evil, violent men do.

They continually gather for war,
And sharpen their tongues like a serpent,
The poison of asps is under their lips,
To Sheol and the pit they should be sent.

Keep me O Lord from wicked hands,
Preserve me from violent men,
They purpose to make my steps stumble,
Save me O Lord from them.

As for the head of those who surround me,
Let the evil of their lips cover them,
Let them be cast into deep pits of fire,
So they cannot rise from there, those men."

PSALM 141

"Lord I cry out to You, make haste to me,
Give ear to my voice when I cry to You,
Let my prayer be before You as incense,
As with lifted hands praise You I do.

Set a guard O Lord over my mouth,
Keep watch over my lips for me,
Do not let my heart incline to do evil,
With evil men working iniquity.

Let the righteous one strike me,
And let him rebuke me too,
It shall be a kindness like precious oil,
Refuse it my head will not do.

My prayer still is against the wicked,
I hate all their wicked deeds,
But my eyes are on You O Lord my God,
You are my refuge and supply all my needs."

PSALM 142

"With my mouth I cry to the Lord,
I make supplication with my voice,
I pour out my complaint before Him,
Because my troubles give me no choice.

You are my refuge and my portion,
In the land of the living hear my cry,
Look on my right hand and see O Lord,
They that secretly snared me I cannot deny.

Deliver me from my persecutors,
For they are much stronger than I,
Bring my soul out of this prison,
To save myself I am not able even to try."

PSALM 143

"Hear my prayer O Lord,
In Your faithfulness answer me,
Do not enter into judgement with Your servant,
For in Your sight no righteous living do You see.

For the enemy has persecuted my soul,
He has crushed my life to the ground,
He has made me dwell in darkness,
Where no salvation for me is found.

I remember the days of old O Lord,
As I meditate on Your works too,
I muse on the works of Your hands,
As I spread out my hands to You.

Answer me quickly O Lord my spirit fails,
Do not hide Your face from me,
Lest I be like those who go down to the pit,
Let Your loving kindness always be.

Deliver me O Lord from my enemies,
For I shelter and trust in only You,
Teach me to do Your will for You are my God,
Your Spirit is full of goodness,
Like all the works that You do."

PSALM 144

"Blessed be the Lord my Rock,
His loving kindness is a fortress to me,
He is my high tower and deliverer,
My refuge and shield He will always be.

Lord what is man that You so know him,
Or the son of man that he is on Your mind?
Man is just like a passing shadow,
He is just a breath, what in him do You find?

Bow down Your heavens O Lord,
Bow them down Lord and come down,
Touch mountains and they will make fire,
Flash lightening and scatter them around.

Stretch out Your hand from above,
From great waters rescue me,
And from the hand of those foreigners,
For they are a lying enemy.

I will sing a new song to You,
O God on a harp of ten strings I will sing,
Praises to the one who gives us salvation,
Who delivered His servant David the king.

Rescue me and deliver me from the enemy,
Who always speaks a lying word,
That our families may always be free,

And filled with Your abundance O Lord."

PSALM 145

"I will exalt You O God my King,
Forever and ever bless Your name,
Every day I will bless You,
For Your greatness is always the same.

Generations shall praise You,
They shall declare Your mighty acts,
I will meditate on Your glory O Lord,
That Your works are wondrous is a fact.

I will speak of Your awesomeness,
And I shall declare your greatness too,
They will always remember Your goodness,
And all the marvellous things that You do.

All Your works shall praise You,
And Your saints will bless You too,
They shall speak of Your Kingdom,
And tell of the great power that belongs to You.

The eyes of all people look to You,
Then You O Lord supply all their need,
You open Your hand and fill them,
So in abundance they will all feed.

The Lord is righteous in all His ways,
His works are filled with His grace,
He answers all who call on Him,

And He puts their enemies into disgrace."

PSALM 146

"Praise the Lord O my soul,
While I live I will praise the Lord,
I will sing praise while I have my being,
I will always praise God for His word.

Do not put your trust in princes,
Nor in the useless help of man,
When the spirit departs he returns to earth,
Then nothing becomes of his plan.

Happy is he who has God for his help,
The God of Jacob will help you,
For He has made the heavens and earth,
And He made all of us too.

He made the seas and all that is in them,
He gave food to the hungry too,
He gave freedom to the prisoners,
What more could He do for you?

The Lord opens the eyes of the blind,
He raises all who are feeling low,
The Lord loves all of the righteous,
And makes everyone's troubles go."

PSALM 147

"It is good to sing praises to our God,
For pleasant and beautiful is praise,
Sing to the Lord with thanksgiving,
Praise and worship to Him raise.

The Lord builds up Jerusalem,
He gathers up all their outcasts,
He heals the broken hearted, binds their wounds,
And even knows when they are joyful at last.

Sing to the Lord with thanksgiving,
Who covers the heavens with clouds,
He prepares rain for the whole earth,
So that grass grows on mountains like shrouds.

He does not delight in a horse's strength,
And takes no pleasure in the legs of man,
The Lord takes pleasure in those who fear Him,
And in all those who believe in His plan.

Praise the Lord O Jerusalem,
Praise Your God O Zion,
For He has strengthened your gates bars,
And fills you with the wheat you rely on.

He sends out His commands to the earth,
He scatters the frost like ashes on snow,
He casts out His hail like large morsels,

And causes His winds to blow.

Who can stand before His cold?
He causes the waters to flow,
He sends out His words and melts them,
And once more His winds do blow."

PSALM 148

"Praise the Lord from the heavens,
Praise Him in the heights too,
Praise Him all you stars of light,
Praise Him all of you.

Let them praise the name of the lord,
He commanded and created all of them,
He established them forever and ever,
He made a decree that will stay until the end.

Praise the Lord from the earth,
You great creatures of the seas,
Fire and hail, snow and clouds,
Stormy winds fulfilling His words, so they do not cease.

Fruitful trees and all cedars,
Beasts, cattle and all creeping things,
Flying fowl and all the peoples,
Princes, judges and kings.

Young men and maidens,
Children and also old men,
Let them all praise the Lord,
For His name is exalted by them.

His glory is above the heavens,
And also far above the earth,
The people of Israel who are near Him,

Praise and worship God for His worth."

PSALM 149

"Praise the Lord all you lands,
In their Maker let Israel rejoice,
Let the children of Zion be joyful in their King,
Let all praise the Lord God with one voice.

Let them praise His name with the dance,
And sing with the timbrel and harp too,
The Lord will beautify His people,
And take pleasure in all that they do.

Let the saints be joyful in glory,
Let them on their beds sing aloud,
With the high praises of God in their mouth,
Making a joyful sound all around.

Let them give the Lord high praises,
With a two edged sword in their hand,
To execute judgement on the nations,
To bind up the kings of their land."

PSALM 150

"Praise God in His sanctuary,
Praise Him for His mighty acts too,
Praise Him according to His greatness,
And for all of His goodness to you.

Praise Him with the trumpet sound,
Praise Him with strings and lute,
Praise Him with the clashing of cymbals,
Let all praise Him without any dispute,
Let everything that has breath praise the Lord."

Praise the Lord Amen!!!!!

A MESSAGE FROM TRISH

On writing and reading the psalms, I saw the heart felt cries to the Lord by so many different people.

David was so poetical, Asaph, well to me he was trying to be like David and nearly succeeding.

The sons of Korah, I thought did not really know how merciful God was at that time in the history of the Jews.

I believe too that some were from Moses himself.

What I got from the books was different ways that we can cry out to God and get an answer every time, because God looks at the heart and not whether you have been clever in speech or writing.

We have to be genuine in our love and worship to the Lord God, whether we be kings, priests, servants or poor beggar.

With a pure heart we are all the same to our loving God who never changes.

He was the same then as He is now and forever will be. Amen.

A MESSAGE FOR
THE READER

I do pray that you have been blessed by reading my book and that you will seek Jesus for yourself if you don't already know Him.

'For God so loved the world that He gave His only Son, that all may have eternal life.' (John 3:16)

The sins of the whole world have been forgiven because Jesus paid the price for them all on the cross.
All we have to do is believe and receive this free gift of Salvation.

This is all I had to do to be born again and filled with the Holy Spirit.

God did not point my sins out to me, but when I received His love, I knew I was a sinner but I had been washed clean and was free to have felowship with Father God for eternity.

I pray this for you too dear reader.

God bless you,

Trish

BOOKS BY THIS AUTHOR

The Gospel Of Matthew In Rhyme

The Bible has most of it's poetry in the Hebrew of the Old Testament. There are the 'Poetic Books' of Job, Psalms, Proverbs, Song of Songs, Ecclesiastes and Lamentations.There are also great sections of poetry in the prophetic books, such as Isaiah.Anything that helps us read God's word today is to be encouraged.In this book, Trish has wonderfully put together the Gospel of Matthew into poetic form.

Trish's Treasures In Rhyme

Inspired by the Holy Spirit, Trish's rhymes are beautifully written as she brings the scriptures alive as well as her own personal treasures. A wonderful book to read and bless you.

From The Gospel Of John In Rhyme

I was so blessed by the reception of my first book 'The Gospel of Matthew in Rhyme' that when it was suggested I undertake the Gospel of John too, I just couldn't say no.I began writing Christian rhymes as a way to encourage people and introduce them into reading the bible for themselves.Why not pick up a bible with this book and see how I did.God bless all who read it.

Printed in Great Britain
by Amazon

81739293R00149